J Tandy
Xmas 1977.
from M.C.W.T.S.

The Working Trial Dog

The Working Trial Dog

PETER LEWIS

Photographs by Michael Jones

POPULAR DOGS
London

Popular Dogs Publishing Company Ltd
3 Fitzroy Square, London W1

An imprint of the Hutchinson Publishing Group

London Melbourne Sydney Auckland
Wellington Johannesburg and agencies
throughout the world

First published 1977

Set in Monotype Garamond

Printed in Great Britain by
The Anchor Press Ltd and bound by
Wm Brendon & Son Ltd
both of Tiptree, Essex

ISBN 0 09 131860 2

To Bill,
a good pupil and
an excellent teacher

Contents

Illustrations

In the text

Author's introduction

The dog is known as 'Man's Best Friend' although recent years have seen a growing anti-dog lobby with the media very quick to publicize alarmist stories about savage or disease-carrying dogs. Sadly it is true that a minority of so-called dog lovers do not accept the responsibilities involved with being a dog owner, inflicting their dog and its habits on anyone who gets in its way. Amongst other things, responsible dog ownership must include training. Once it is understood how a dog's mind works training is a question of commonsense applied to dog training principles.

The training methods described in this book are based upon channelling the puppy in the right direction from the beginning, thereby ensuring that the dog does not develop bad habits which may later necessitate corrective training. Once this becomes necessary the trainer risks apprehension and a subsequent unwilling worker with all but a very hard natured dog.

It would be wrong for me to write a book such as this without acknowledging a debt of gratitude which I owe to Charlie Wyant who taught me much about control or obedience training. Whilst he has never seriously been involved in Working Trials, many of the training principles that he taught me can be applied to this sport. I am also grateful to Michael Jones and his wife Janet for the photographic session.

Man's best friend becomes an even greater friend if well trained, and it is my hope that this book will help those with little knowledge of training principles to own a better trained pet, and at the same time serve as an introduction to one of the types of dog training competitions known as Working Trials.

I

Selection and education

CHOICE OF A SUITABLE DOG

Let us assume the decision has been made to obtain a dog, either purely as a pet, or for the express purpose of competing at Working Trials. Whilst in both cases substantial training is advisable, if competition is contemplated then training becomes essential. Any animal training requires a degree of patience, and it is quite surprising to find that people who are normally impatient in their everyday lives can become patient dog trainers providing that they have the dedication and will to succeed. There are many attributes required to make a successful team of man and dog, but in my opinion they can be brought down to three basic ingredients. The right person, with the right knowledge, with the right material. The right person I can have no control over, but would be a person suited to a particular dog who, when absent from his or her instructor, has the ability to interpret today's training problem set by the dog into an answer from previous instruction.

The right knowledge is something which this book aims to help provide the prospective dog handler. The right material can be much more tricky than most people imagine and it is usually the first mistake the beginner makes, and it is probably the biggest mistake of all.

First we must consider which breed is to be favoured. The most predominant breed to be found at Working Trials has always been the Alsatian, or German Shepherd Dog, as most fanciers of this breed prefer to call it. The police force have a greater number of Alsatians (German Shepherd Dogs) than any other breed for they have found by experience that the Alsatian is the breed most suited to the varied type of work required from the trained patrol dog. The expense of training a police dog is considerable, so therefore economics play a part in determining which breed the police use, one of these economies being a long working life. Stamina is also a necessity and the fit Alsatian possesses this as well. A good retrieve instinct and a keen nose for tracking are necessary, and most Alsatians are not to be found wanting in this department. Whilst this breed has a reputation for being fierce, they can be very gentle, the former unfair reputation being perpertrated and maintained by the media in the interests of saleable copy. The Alsatian is no more fierce than any other breed, but such a reputation is turned to advantage by the police. The production of the police dog and handler amongst a crowd of rowdies is very often a sufficient deterrent against lawlessness. The Alsatian with good temperament is often excellent material for being trained to detect, pursue and detain the criminal. One of the problems with this breed has been its tremendous popularity since the war, and it is now something of a lottery to be able to purchase a puppy which will grow to be a bold dog of sound temperament, free from hereditary defects.

This problem is not confined to the Alsatian, for many of the popular breeds have temperament and hereditary defect problems. Ancestry of the Labrador Retriever requires careful scrutiny prior to purchasing in an effort to minimize these possibilities. For nosework alone, a good Labrador Retriever is very hard to beat. In the right hands they make superb tracking dogs, but, with rare exceptions, they do not excel in some of the control exercises. As most civilians taking part in Working Trials only compete in the tracking stakes, then a Labrador is a good choice. The bitch of this breed is often a far better training proposition as the male can be over-sexed and strong-willed, and therefore, if not sympathetically handled, an unwilling worker can be the result. It would be wrong to say that the Labrador will not work if bullied, for whilst this is very true such a statement implies that other breeds can be successfully bullied into working. In truth, a good working dog can never be trained in this manner. The Labrador Retriever has great stamina and endurance and can work all day in cold wind and rain, but if not exercised he becomes lazy. His appealing eyes will often ensure a regular supply of tit-bits, which combined with laziness, is a short cut to unnecessary obesity. Few pet dog owners realize that it is cruel to allow a dog to become overweight. They seem to think that a continual supply of food several times a day is a sign of their affection for the animal. I wonder if they ever stop to think that they may be sending the dog to an early grave.

The Border Collie is another breed that makes a good tracking dog, and one keen and willing to learn what is required. The average Collie has tremendous enthusiasm for work and this has been brought about by the fact that shepherds were not rich men and could only afford to keep dogs that were going to earn their keep, any others were put down. This continual process has left us with a breed whose enthusiasm for work cannot be surpassed by any other breed. Like the Labrador, the Border Collie is at home in the cold and wet. Of all the breeds suitable for Working Trials the Collie is the most agile, which means on average a longer working life, for many of the other breeds are prematurely retired from competition because of agility problems. The Border Collie in the right hands can really excel on the obedience and control exercises, giving sparkling performances if correctly trained. In recent years more Collies have been seen competing successfully at Working Trials, but the reader should not make the mistake of thinking that it is only necessary to purchase a Collie to win prizes, for they are only as good as their handler, and in the wrong hands they can be a liability. For the same reason a Border Collie is not a good choice as just a pet, he needs to be worked so that natural enthusiasm for work does not turn to vice.

The Dobermann can make a good tracking dog but is better handled with a mixture of firmness and understanding, and being an active and spirited type of dog, he must be kept under control. Originally the Dobermann was bred as a strong and well-made guard and companion dog, and therefore notices everything that is going on within sight and earshot. From what he sees and hears he will very often make his own decisions and decide on a course of action without waiting for the handler's instructions. This initiative can be useful to the patrol dog, but also can at times be a liability. If handled too severely or if confused, the Dobermann can go off on a gallop, which at first sight seems to be blatant disobedience, but this is where understanding for the breed is necessary.

The Dobermann has little trouble with the agility exercises, but care should be taken with the bitch who will need a slower build-up to the six-foot scale than her male counterpart. The ten-minute down stay can present a problem for varying reasons. The Dobermann's lack of hair gives little underbody and leg protection and therefore cold and wet weather can mean that the dog is extremely uncomfortable, or his attachment for his owner is such that the inactivity and boredom of the stay exercise is soon dispensed with in favour of rejoining his handler. Careful and patient training can overcome these possibilities so that the handler has a reliable dog.

Rottweilers originate from Germany where primarily they were used as cattle dogs. It is a strong breed with good stamina, but being a heavy dog it is expensive to feed and can have agility problems, particularly towards the end of its working life. Whilst the Rottweiler is not usually the smartest of breeds in the control work, he is no more difficult to train than other breeds, and can, to a certain extent, be described as naturally obedient and faithful. Nosework presents no problem to the well trained and handled Rottweiler.

Groenendaels, or Belgian Shepherd Dogs, could well grow in popularity for Trials work in the coming years, and in many respects they are not unlike their neighbour, the Alsatian. Sheep herders kept this breed to protect and to herd their flocks for they are an intelligent breed that accept training. Generally speaking they are of good temperament and are able to work in extremes of temperature. There is nothing in the Working Trials schedule that would prove exceptionally difficult to a Groenendael.

Boxers have been worked with success in Trials for many years. They make a good patrol dog and have, over the years, been used at various times for police work by different countries. They are an active, well-muscled and compact dog, that descend from hunting dogs used in Germany during the middle ages. Generally speaking they are reliable and sensible with children, and to be at their best, should never be allowed to become overweight. Well trained, they have no difficulty with nosework, and the agility exercises present few problems for them.

There are other breeds that could well excel at Trials work, but the prospective handler must realize that to reach the top stakes a breed of at least medium size is necessary, for the schedule demands that all breeds should scale six feet from the Working Dog Stake onwards. There are, however, two stakes below this one where the height and lengths of the jump are determined by the size of the dog, and owners of smaller breeds may well get a lot of satisfaction training their dogs to these standards.

The prospective dog owner must also consider the problem of whether to purchase a dog or a bitch. It must be remembered that not only is it unfair to competing dogs to work a bitch in season, but Kennel Club rules forbid it. A bitch is generally in season twice a year for a three-week period, but it is probably true to say that she is less easily distracted than the male and can therefore be a better training proposition for the civilian. For example the most outstanding Labradors to compete in Working Trials have been bitches. However, a dog is generally stronger and has less trouble with the agility exercises. He is also likely to be more aggressive as a guard or patrol dog.

Over the years I have been involved with many dog training obedience classes. Pet dog owners enrol for these classes, hoping to be helped with problems of training their chosen pet. In so many instances it has been sad to watch a handler struggling with a dog to which he or she is entirely unsuited. A strong, large, bold dog will require a strong, firm handler, but so often a diminutive lady of questionable strength will attempt to train such a dog. I have also seen a strong male manual worker with a shy miniature poodle, and that combination was doomed from the start. A nervous handler can aggravate similiar tendencies in any breed of dog. One of the fastest reacting breeds is the Border Collie who requires speedy reactions from his handler. Because so much of their work is executed with panache, many people think they are easily trained. In fact a Collie with a slow plodding insensitive handler is a disaster, and a quick reacting impatient handler can be set upon a collision course with a slower plodding breed.

The ideal is to match the dog and handler for various qualities so that they have every chance of becoming a team, making the best use of the qualities at both ends of the lead. No dog is perfect, and even more so, as the human can never fully understand the canine, no handler acquires perfection. A good team can help each other, and a poor team will wander in the wilderness.

The very nature of Working Trials demand certain qualities of those who wish to succeed in competition. It is a long route to the top requiring much perseverance and patience. The handler will require a reasonable degree of fitness to be in a position to traverse difficult ground and to lay and work tracks in all weathers, so that when one feels more comfortable by the fire, if training is due, determination and the will to succeed must triumph.

The very nature of the sport means that the prospective trainer needs to have access to reasonably large amounts of land. Whilst a half-mile track can be easily laid in an eight-acre field, the dog should be trained on a variety of land surfaces, but this aspect of training is covered more fully in later chapters. Opportunities for training the dog have also to be taken into account, particularly during the initial stages. Whilst many of the basic control exercises can be taught at home, nosework and sendaways require larger amounts of land than are to be found in most people's back gardens. As travelling to and from the training land has to be taken into consideration, the time element takes on even greater importance.

When a dog is being taught any new exercise he needs to be trained far more frequently than perhaps twice at the weekend. In this respect, ladies who are not part of the family bread-winning team, have greater opportunities for training. Handlers who have previously trained for Obedience Competitions have certain advantages and disadvantages. Whilst, at first sight, control exercises look almost identical to some of those to be found in the Obedience Schedule (S2) the complete reliance on the handler that the successful obedience dog needs is a hinderance for the Trials dog. A dog that has become over-submissive to his handler will not easily be able to work on his own initiative, which becomes so important with the nosework. Therefore a slightly different approach to Trials control work is required. One which gives the handler the necessary control, but at the same time allows the dog the freedom to work happily at a distance from the handler who has taken over the post of pack leader. For example, heelwork requires complete reliance by the dog on his handler, and therefore a certain degree of submission. If this submission is too great, the dog will be bewildered once it is at a distance from the handler, and is then expected to work on its own initiative. This I believe to be one of the main reasons why some dogs will not leave their handler further than a few feet away whilst working the search area.

Having decided upon the breed, the next move should be to contact a reputable breeder, or to seek advice from experienced people who handle your chosen breed in Trials. There are many pitfalls here. An illustrious pedigree covered in red ink is not going to guarantee a good working dog. For example, a dog has a better chance of being a possible worker if it has come from working stock. Half a dozen or more breed champions in the pedigree may mean there is a chance of a good-looking dog, but it will not indicate potential working capabilities.

One of the greatest problems facing breeders today is hereditary defects. Again a dog with a good working background is not necessarily a guarantee that he will not be suffering from one or more of the many defects affecting pedigree dogs. Whilst I do not feel it is right for a book of this sort to go into veterinary detail, a brief description of some of these defects may make the prospective purchaser a little more aware of some of the questions that need to be asked of a breeder. Hip dysplasia is, as the title implies, a defect of the hips. Alsatians and Labradors seriously affected can be a real problem to the Working Trial enthusiast, for HD will mean agility problems. Indeed, a dog badly affected should not be jumped, and several good dogs have been prematurely retired from competition because of HD.

Progressive retinal atrophy (PRA) is more commonly known as night blindness. Of these two words, the latter is more correct than the former. Border Collies were badly affected at one time, but a vigilant campaign by the International Sheepdog Society has done much to drastically reduce its incidence.

Epilepsy, whilst well known in humans, is not usually associated with the dog. However, this has occurred in many breeds, and the prospective purchaser should avoid purchasing any dog where epilepsy has been established in its ancestry. Dogs with this defect would not normally be a sound proposition for work, although fits only occur during a dog's inactive periods. However medication can successfully control the problem.

Entropion, or ingrowing eyelashes, is a defect that can occur in Labradors. It has only recently come to the fore, yet I can remember in 1949 as a lad we looked after two black Labradors, mother and daughter, and the mother was badly affected.

One of the problems in writing a chapter of this sort is to do so without making it appear that the beginner has little chance of purchasing the right breed with the right temperament, in a perfect state of health. It is possible, and if this chapter stops just a few people 'leaping into the deep end' without much thought, then it has served its purpose. Probably the best advice I can give is to suggest that the prospective purchaser attends one or two Trials and talks to people who have the experience and who should be able to give advice. Your puppy will grow to be a dog, hopefully with a life span of many years. It is therefore prudent to avoid a bad choice at the outset.

Having chosen the breed and located a litter of puppies, make an appointment with the breeder to call and see them in order to observe the puppies in their own environment. Note carefully which puppies come bounding out to greet you for these are more likely to grow up bold and fearless. Beware of the shy little fellow in the corner with the sad expression on his face for this may be a sign that shyness will be with him for the rest of his life. Here lady buyers are the worst offenders for their maternal instinct often convinces them that he needs a friend.

We can assume that by now the choice has been narrowed to just one or two of the litter. The next point to look for is a strong retrieve instinct, for much of the dog's future working life will be based upon the retrieve, and even other exercises that it will be taught which bear no relation to the retrieve can be made pleasurable to the dog by using the retrieve as a reward for work well done. Obviously it is unlikely that any of the pups will actually go out, retrieve and deliver to hand, but it does happen. One is looking only for the instinct, and this is quite easy to observe. Take any small object, which should not be too hard, and throw it a few feet making sure the puppies see what is happening. As a general guide, the puppies that rush straight out to investigate the object have a retrieve instinct, and these are the ones from which your final choice should be made.

You must now make your financial arrangements with the breeder, obtain the puppy's pedigree, and check whether the breeder is registering the whole litter with the Kennel Club. If not, one can register the pup purchased by making an application to the Kennel Club who will send the necessary forms. Registration is essential if you are going to enter any competition held under the rules and regulations of the Kennel Club, and Working Trials are no exception.

Before leaving with a puppy, check the feeding details and make sure that either there is someone with you to carry the puppy on their lap in the car, or that there is a suitable box to put the puppy in. Do not forget that from now on you are responsible for the association of ideas that the puppy may develop, and as it may well spend much of its life travelling in a motor car, the initial journey should be as pleasurable as possible.

PUPPY EDUCATION

I am a great believer in channelling the pup in the right direction from the time he arrives home. This cannot be called training in the correct sense of the word, but without doubt a lot of hard work and heartache at a later stage can be avoided by making use of the work it is necessary to do for the puppy right from the start. For example, shortly after arriving home it will be time to feed the puppy and this feeding time can be the beginning of a recall, a sendaway, or both. I prefer to start with the sendaway which may sound a little strange for it is one of the more advanced exercises and a little more difficult to teach an adult dog. One should really try to achieve an association of ideas right from the start.

With the feeding dish in one hand, tuck the puppy under the other arm (with any luck he will be struggling to get to his food), make sure that he sees you place the dish on the ground, then move back approximately ten feet and as the puppy is lowered to the ground let go and quietly say 'Away'. The puppy will run happily to the food and before very long will be more than willing to move away from the handler on this command. Repeat this every feeding time until you are sure that the puppy understands the command, and when at a later date it is time to teach him the sendaway as required in competition, you will find that the hardest part of the exercise has already been learned by the puppy, i.e. the ability to leave you on command.

Feeding time can also be used as the basis of a recall. Once the food is prepared, take it to the feeding place making any sound that is interesting to the puppy. As the puppy reaches you, place the food dish on the ground by your feet and praise him. The selected sound should always be the same, with the puppy's name interspersed between. Gradually the command 'Come' can be introduced and as he progresses you can drop the sound and just use his name plus the command. Again this is not training in the correct sense of the word but rather channelling him in the right direction.

If it is decided to use feeding time for the basis of the sendaway then tit-bits can be used instead of food as the beginning of the recall. Use the procedure described above and as soon as the puppy reaches you, let him have the tit-bit and praise him. Gradually stop giving the tit-bit, relying instead on the praise. Whatever happens do not get to the stage where the puppy will *only* come for the food. It is an interim measure to build an association of the command with pleasure. If these procedures are followed, when the time comes to teach the exercise properly, 90 per cent of it has already been learned and all the pulling and pushing on a lead can be avoided which so often is the cause of apprehension associated with the command. The net result of apprehension is a slow unwilling dog. The aim must be not only a trained dog but a happy and willing one.

There are hundreds of dog training clubs in the country all performing a useful task for the local community by teaching people how to train dogs. Unfortunately, by the time the owners and dogs reach these clubs the dog is already out of hand and it is more a case of corrective measures being necessary than teaching the handler to train a dog that has not yet developed bad habits. The two most common faults that induce people to join a dog training club are pulling on the lead and failing to come when called. I have already shown how to avoid the latter fault by starting off in the correct manner, and the other fault will be dealt with later.

This chapter has so far been devoted solely to the puppy, but for the owner of an adult dog who has already developed these bad habits, the later chapters will indicate how to proceed.

Dogs are sensitive to many things. One of them is noise, and if the dog is to compete in Working Trials it needs to be steady to the sound of a gunshot. Obviously one does not obtain a gun and start blasting away over the young puppy's head, but it is possible to introduce sudden noises from the beginning. Start with soft noises and over a period of time as each noise is accepted with confidence, the stage is reached where the sudden bang of the dustbin lid over the puppy's head can be accomplished without him taking more than casual notice. This is all that is required at this stage for the actual gunshot can be introduced during later training.

Do not forget to introduce the puppy to traffic at the earliest possible age. Since we live in the age of the motor car he will frequently have to contend with this noise. Do not take the puppy straight to the kerb of a main road and frighten him with the thundering noises of heavy lorries, but rather begin with light traffic at a reasonable distance, gradually building up to heavy traffic over a period of time. Remember too that a dog during its life may well spend many hours travelling in a car and it is therefore wise to train the dog for car travel. The way to do this is to start at home with the car stationary in the drive. It may sound peculiar but a dog needs to be taught how to get in and out of a car in an orderly fashion. For example you do not want a dog that rushes out immediately the car pulls up. He should not get out until you give him a command to do so, for sometimes you will wish to open the door or tailgate in a busy street without fear of the dog lunging past in his haste to get out. A dog also needs to be taught to lie quietly during the journey, and again this can be taught at home, building up from a stationary car with the engine off and progressing to a stationary car with the engine on. When the dog is steady and reliable you can move away for the first time, preferably with someone else driving so that you can concentrate your attention on this part of the training.

2

Training for control

GENERAL

Control is so often neglected in Working Trials, taking second place to nosework training. One has only to watch this group of exercises at a Trial to see many dogs who are not up to the required standard. Yet only 70 per cent of the allocated marks are necessary to qualify in this group. Assuming that a dog does not fail in the ten-minute down exercise then qualification on control should really be a formality and not the subject of fear as it is for some competitors. It seems a terrible waste when a judge has watched a dog complete the nosework with exceptional expertise and then has to fail it on a relatively simple exercise. Many a Working Trial Certificate has been lost by poor obedience or control when perhaps with a little more effort during the dog's early training days, these exercises could have been mastered once and for all, leaving the handler reasonably confident of good marks in competition.

I have always felt that the overall standard of control leaves a lot to be desired and I know there are some judges who share this view. The last thing I would like to see in Trials is the stereotype or military precision seen at Obedience Shows, but at the same time there is a lot of room for improvement. Don't get the impression that I am against Obedience Shows, as for a number of years I have been both a competitor and judge at this sport and have enjoyed it as much as Trials. Obedience Shows as they are today are purely a circus trick and the winner is the dog which performs with the greatest degree of perfection. Generally speaking there is not a lot of room for variation in the test as defined by the rules, and societies are restricted with the space that can be allocated to each class. The control or obedience sections of Working Trials very often feature variations in the test from Trial to Trial, such as the heelwork being tested through the spectators or around the parked cars, or 150 yard sendaways to a bush or a hole in a fence. Obedience Shows do not on the whole have sufficient space for tests of this nature. An explanation of this is that whilst Working Trials and Obedience Shows have similiar exercises in the schedule, the way a judge sets and marks the test in both sports varies considerably, and long may they continue to do so. Trials are one thing and Obedience Shows another. They both have much to commend and both have their faults.

Competitors in the two different spheres of training should be tolerant towards each other and not condemn the other's sport as sometimes happens. Nevertheless, where Working Trials are concerned, there is a great deal of room for improvement of the handling in this part of the schedule.

Serious training should commence as soon as possible and the time to start depends entirely on the nature of the puppy. Some dogs can be started at three months and others need to be left until they are much older. I do however like to have a puppy carry out the basic control exercises reasonably well by the time it is six to nine months of age – the basic exercises being heelwork on and off the lead, recall to handler, retrieve of the dumb-bell, and the sit and down stay. The yardstick to use to see if a dog is ready to accept serious training of any exercise is when he can be taught with a very minimum amount of correction, relying instead on encouragement and praise. If at any time it is necessary to use too much correction, then do not attempt to go any further. It is preferable to wait until the dog will accept teaching without the use of force of any kind. Correction and force refer to the use of the lead in conjunction with the check chain which is very often necessary with an older dog that has developed a will of his own and is trying to exert that will over the handler. There is a school of thought which says a puppy should be left until much older before serious training commences as starting too early destroys the dog's initiative. This view has merit it is true, but provided it is only a question of teaching and not of continual correction, then the earlier the start is made the better. Generally speaking, the younger the dog is, the more readily he accepts training, having developed fewer bad habits which need correction. However, it must be emphasized that each dog is different and there are no hard and fast rules as to the correct age to start. The handler, or someone with considerable experience, must be the judge of that.

Before training is undertaken some equipment must be acquired by the handler, and details of this can be found in Chapter 5.

THE RECALL

If the natural method of teaching the puppy to come when called as described in the first chapter is successful, then the recall as an exercise can be taught very easily and very quickly. By now the dog should come bounding up when called by name followed by the word 'Come', still using the interesting sound if necessary. A recall as such has already been achieved and only the beginning and the end of the exercise need to be tidied. Before the puppy is introduced to the check chain and lead, he can be taught to sit still, thereby enabling the handler to leave the puppy so that he can be recalled. Very gently push down on the puppy's hindquarters giving the command 'Sit' simultaneously. Immediately he responds praise him but do not give more praise than necessary or he will not remain sitting. Move the hand away from his hindquarters gradually, praising at the same time, but be ready to return it should there be any attempt to move, repeating the command 'Sit'. Very slowly and gradually move away from the puppy, a few inches at a time and then a few feet, until after several lessons it is possible to retreat about ten or twelve feet. It will be noted that I have not suggested the use of the command 'Stay' for I prefer to use the command 'Sit' if the dog is subsequently to be asked to move from a distance, and 'Sit – Stay' only if I intend to return to the dog.

When the dog is steady in the sit position and you have moved back to the required distance, with the feet placed six to nine inches apart pause for a few seconds and then, bringing both hands simultaneously together to the groin, give the dog's name and the command 'Come'. As the dog reaches you, gently but firmly push the hindquarters down so that he sits, and sits *straight*. Immediately praise him as he responds and if his puppy recall training included the ocasional tit-bit when he sat straight, give him this tit-bit and praise him. Should he at any time move before the command, return to the puppy and replace him in the exact position in which you left him. If this is not done you will have a dog that anticipates the recall.

When the puppy is reliable enough for you to be able to turn your back on him and walk away, as you turn to face him remember to allow a pause before calling him or he may associate the act of turning to face him as a signal to come. Be careful with your arms for you are also using them for a signal, and if they unconsciously flap around as you turn to face him, he may think he is being called. You may well scold him for moving when in fact he is doing his best to please, and then you are not helping to build confidence which is essential with any exercise. Never at any time scold him when he comes to you or you may build into him an association that it is unpleasant to return to the handler. It is far better always to praise him when he comes no matter how angry you are with him for a previous misconduct. Remember a dog only associates his immediate actions with correction or reward.

You will note that I have emphasized '*sit straight*' for it is so easy to teach the dog to sit at the correct angle whilst he is a puppy and easily manoeuvred into position. It is also just as easy incorrectly to teach the puppy to sit at any angle by praising even when he is not sitting straight. If you make sure that his behind is placed straight in front of you every time, then you will never suffer from continual crooked sits which look untidy and are often penalized, particularly in the CD Stake.

You should now be the owner of a dog that will recall immediately the command and hand signal to the groin is given. In future, the act of placing the hands in the groin is a signal to the dog to come and present in front – be it for a recall or a retrieve.

So much for the recall, for in all probability the teaching is over and done with in a few lessons provided you started in the right way. Yet the average pet dog owner finds great difficulty in getting the dog to come when called. If there is a recall problem, then other methods must be adopted, necessitating the use of the check chain and lead. Assuming that the dog has not yet worn a collar and lead, gradually introduce him to these two training aids. Provided care is taken not to hurt the dog whilst still a puppy, put on the check chain, which should be large enough to avoid a struggle when fitting it over the head and ears, and when pulled up tight there should be three or four inches of spare chain. There are two ways the chain can be worn. Only one of these two ways is correct (see photograph and Figure 7) and if used the wrong way, the check chain only operates as a choke and becomes useless as a training aid.

Once the dog is used to wearing the chain, and this may be after several lessons, clip on a good strong leather lead, preferably with a trigger hook. This lead needs to be three or four feet long to allow sufficient distance between the handler and the dog. In all probability the dog will object to the lead so do not attempt to struggle with him but let him run around with the lead trailing. Repeat this each time until any objections are over and you can hold the lead without him struggling.

Teach the dog to sit still by the same method as described for the puppy without a lead, except that as you press down on his hindquarters with the left hand, hold the lead gently pulled tight in the right hand above his head, giving the command 'Sit' as you do so. Remember to praise the dog immediately you get a response. It is preferable to carry out this manoeuvre with the dog sitting on your left-hand side, and as this is the position in which he must sit for the heelwork exercise, then the only angle to allow him to sit at is straight beside you. If you fail to do this from the beginning then you may inadvertently be teaching the dog untidy crooked sits which will give extra problems when heelwork lessons commence.

When the dog is steady in the sit and you can back off to the end of the lead without him moving, hold the lead in the right hand but have the left hand on the lead as well. Give the lead a jerk so that both hands finish up in the groin, and as you do so call the dog's name followed by the command 'Come'. Gather up the lead as the dog comes towards you so that he has a minimum amount of slack and you have complete control. As he responds, remember to praise him, and when he arrives in front of you place him in the sit position by holding the lead tight with the right hand slightly above his head. At the same time press down with the left hand on his hindquarters and ensure that he is placed in a straight sit. Immediately he sits *praise* him.

You will no doubt have noticed that the word *praise* is used in italics. The reason is that I cannot place sufficient emphasis on

Using feeding time to educate a puppy.
A recall *above*; a sendaway *below*

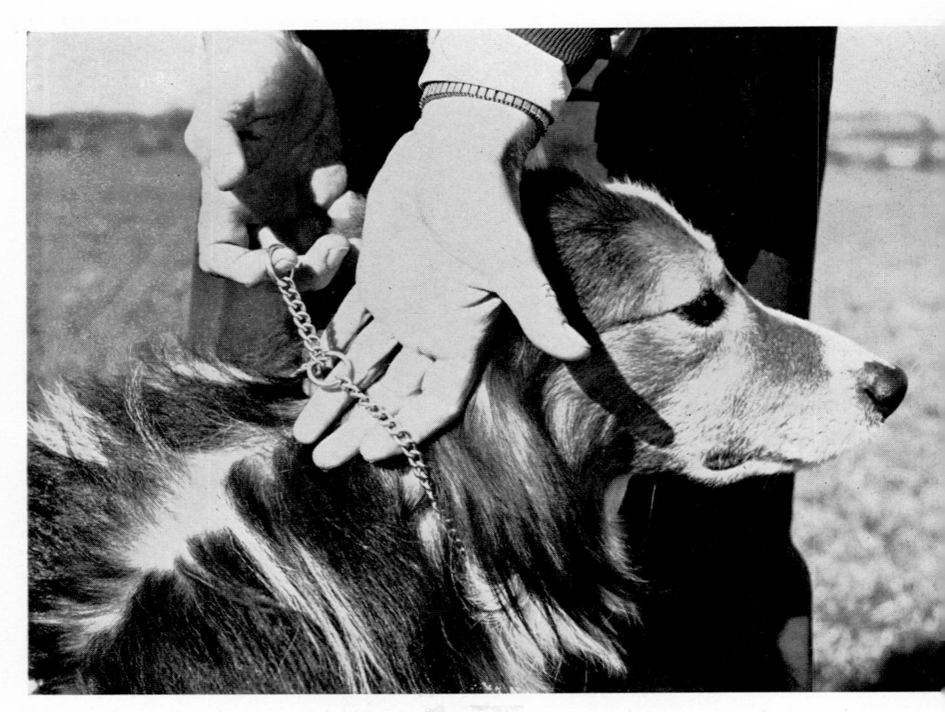

Above. The correct way for a dog to wear the check chain. Note four inches of slack when tightened

Left. Teaching the dog to sit in the heel position

The recall

The immediate down

Teaching the dog to pay attention

praise. It is necessary every time the dog responds to any form of training yet it is amazing how many handlers forget to use it.

THE STAYS AND THE IMMEDIATE DOWN

The sit and down stays, are, on the face of it, the most simple exercises for the dog to learn for they require no action from the dog whatsoever. However, in competition it is amazing how often it is necessary to fail a dog for moving out of the line of dogs or for changing position from the sit to the down, or vice versa. If a dog has been taught correctly from the beginning there should never be any question of his moving out of line unless there are exceptional circumstances such as interference from another dog. The question of the dog changing position is somewhat different for very often a dog left in the sit or down will adopt the opposite position during the exercise. However, in Working Trials the sit stay is only scheduled in the CD Stake but nevertheless it should be mastered.

It is general practice in this stake for the judge to test the dogs in the sit followed immediately by the down. The greatest mistake a handler can make is to train a dog the same way. When practising, never attempt the two exercises consecutively for a dog will build up the association of one exercise following the other. If this happens it is quite easy to see why a dog will for no apparent reason change from the sit to the down position. He is probably quite happy in his own mind that he is not being disobedient, for as far as he is concerned he is doing a stay and is only unsure of which of the two positions he should be in. Should this happen it is pointless to correct the dog on return. Remember he only associates correction and reward with his immediate actions and by the time the handler has returned it is too late. The dog must be caught in the act of moving and the only way to do this is for the handler to go to great lengths to outwit him, giving him the impression that his handler is out of sight in the distance, when in fact he is hidden only a few feet away and in such a way that the dog can be seen but the dog cannot see the handler. A series of small buildings such as sheds, etc, are useful for this purpose, but remember that the wind should not be in the direction of handler to dog. Having left the dog in the sit, move away in a forward direction, and once out of sight double back round the buildings until only a few feet from him. If this manoeuvre is carried out correctly the dog will have quite a surprise when he lies down, thinking that his handler is in the distance when in fact he is close enough to apply correction immediately. The maximum effect must be gained the first time for it is unlikely that a clever dog will be fooled a second time.

It can be assumed that by now the dog has been taught to sit for the recall exercise so it will only be necessary to teach the meaning of 'Sit stay'. Give the command and a hand signal, using the flat of the hand in front of his face and step away with the right foot. The main object now is to build up the dog's confidence, so proceed slowly, starting only a few feet away and over a period of time progress until he can be left sitting for two or three minutes whilst in sight. At this stage the time has come for the handler to move to the out of sight position. It must be stressed that this cannot be rushed and that it may well take many weeks, or even months, to reach this stage. Every time the dog breaks a stay it is a step backwards, but if he only stays for ten seconds before being released, progress has been made.

Until now, no mention has been made of the dog going down on command. It is one of the most important lessons any dog should learn, for if the dog cannot be dropped under almost any circumstances, then there is not complete control. The ability to drop a dog is generally referred to as 'the immediate down' and is an exercise which should be taught as soon as the dog is accustomed to being on a check chain and lead. Hold the handle of the lead in the right hand and manoeuvre into a position where the dog is on the left. Give the command 'down' in a low, firm authoritative tone as the left hand passes down the lead to the chain. When the hand reaches the chain force the dog down, dropping on to the left knee. In all probability he will struggle, but hold him firmly using soothing sounds to ease any fears. If his struggles become violent, repeat the command. Once the struggling has stopped, substitute the left foot for the left hand and slowly stand up. After a few seconds release him and try again. Immediately there is a response, allow him to go down of his own accord without the use of force, but he must go down immediately and quickly and the handler should not accept less. Whatever happens do not fall into the trap of begging the dog to go down. By begging, I mean a handler who requires many commands to drop a dog. When first training never give the command more than twice, for the second command should be accompanied by the act of compelling the dog to the ground. As progress is made, run and play with the dog whilst he is on the lead, suddenly dropping him every now and again until he will drop *immediately* under any circumstances without the application of the lead. Proceed in this manner until he can be dropped at a distance.

With a dog that tries to bite the hand as it slides down the lead to the chain, loop the lead under the left foot just a few inches off the ground. Press down with the foot, pulling the lead up with the right hand, thus forcing the dog down. As this is done give the command. Remember to *praise* immediately he is steady as this will reassure him and let him know that he is doing what is required of him, but excessive praise may excite him into thinking he is being released and he may try to get up. For control reasons the importance of this exercise cannot be over-stressed, but if the advice in Chapter 1 has been followed in teaching a puppy the basis of a sendaway, the dog should go away on command and now also drop on command. It is therefore only necessary to teach the dog to go straight and acquire distance to perfect this advanced exercise. It can be seen at this stage that teaching one basic exercise correctly can make advanced training simple. We can now assume it is possible to give the command 'Down' and the dog will drop instantly.

The procedure for teaching the down stay is now exactly the same as that described for the sit stay, but again it must be stressed, proceed slowly to build the dog's confidence.

Points to remember are:

Do not practise both the sit and down stay consecutively.

Do not correct the dog from a distance for changing his position.

Do not correct the dog when returning to him unless that correction immediately follows a change of position.

Do not keep repeating the command. The second time should be the last accompanied by such action that will ensure subsequent commands are unnecessary.

Praise when the dog responds.

HEELWORK

Heelwork as a competition exercise is best taught early in the young dog's life, but there is a school of thought which says it is best to wait until the puppy has matured before heelwork training commences.

The problem with leaving heelwork until later is that once the puppy has been inoculated against all the various canine diseases he will need to be exercised. This will involve the use of a collar and lead, and if he has not been taught how to behave on a lead, many bad habits can develop which will necessitate correction later. The obvious example is pulling on the lead, which to correct at a later date requires continual jerking of the lead. With a hard type of dog this will not matter too much as he can accept this and still enjoy heelwork. A softer natured dog, however, will only become cowed by the continual jerking and after a while associate the command and the heelwork stance of the handler as something unpleasant, and this will clearly be shown in the style of the dog's heelwork. An example of this is the dog that lags on heelfree. Inevitably this has been brought about by over-use of the lead. Sometimes it is said that this is caused by the boredom of continual repetition of the exercise, but if the dog is taught to enjoy the exercise he will happily train at any time. The way to achieve a happy heelworker is to teach the exercise as something natural so that only a minimum amount of lead handling is necessary and therefore the dog learns by encouragement and praise.

Another mistake to avoid is to allow the dog to sit at anything other than the correct position when halting. During early lessons many handlers are only too pleased that their dog has sat at all, allowing him to sit at any angle and praising him for doing so, for it must be confusing for the dog to be corrected at a later date for sitting crooked when originally this had been accepted by the handler. Continual correction for crooked sits can cause apprehension of the halts and subsequent lagging. It is much easier to teach the dog to sit straight from the beginning of training than it is to correct the fault later.

I prefer to teach heelwork to a dog by first teaching the correct position of sitting on my left side and having his complete attention. In the section on recall training a description was given of how to teach the dog to sit. To begin heelwork training place the dog in the sit position at heel, holding the lead in the right hand and teach the dog to pay attention by using tit-bits or a squeaky toy. As soon as he responds, gently praise him, correcting the dog quietly with the voice the split second his attention is lost, immediately reverting to the incentive again. Start by holding his attention for just a few seconds, then release the dog by playing with him for a few minutes. Go through this procedure several times in any one lesson until over a period of time he will sit at heel and give complete attention on command. Do not attempt any heelwork until attention has been perfected even if it takes many weeks. Never allow the dog to become bored, as playing should be introduced before this stage is reached. If the handler is using tit-bits they should be discontinued as soon as possible to avoid having a dog that will only work for food.

When satisfied that under reasonable circumstances complete attention is achieved, transfer the lead to the left hand which is placed in the groin. Allow only sufficient slack to enable the lead to be tightened by turning the wrist. Give the command for attention and when ready the command 'Heel' and take one pace *only*, stepping off with the left foot. Should attention be lost and the handler be unable to regain it, the dog is not yet ready to move from the sitting position and further lessons are necessary. On the other hand, if the dog's attention is held as one pace is taken, try several paces next time. In all probability, whilst his attention can be held he may resist, necessitating a lot of correction to hold him in the heelwork position. If this is so, do not attempt to correct, but finish the lesson immediately by reverting to play once again. Under these circumstances it is possible that heelwork is being taught before the dog is ready, and therefore the handler should not attempt to teach it until training is accepted with the minimum amount of correction. Rather than a lot of pulling and jerking on the lead whilst the handler attempts to force heelwork from the dog, it is preferable to continue with just the attention exercise. A week or more later the handler can attempt to move off again. If the dog still resists, then unclip the lead and try again at a later date. On one of the occasions when attempting heelwork, the handler will find that the occasional flick of the lead by sharply turning the left wrist, plus commands and encouragement, will be all that is necessary to keep the dog happily at heel without

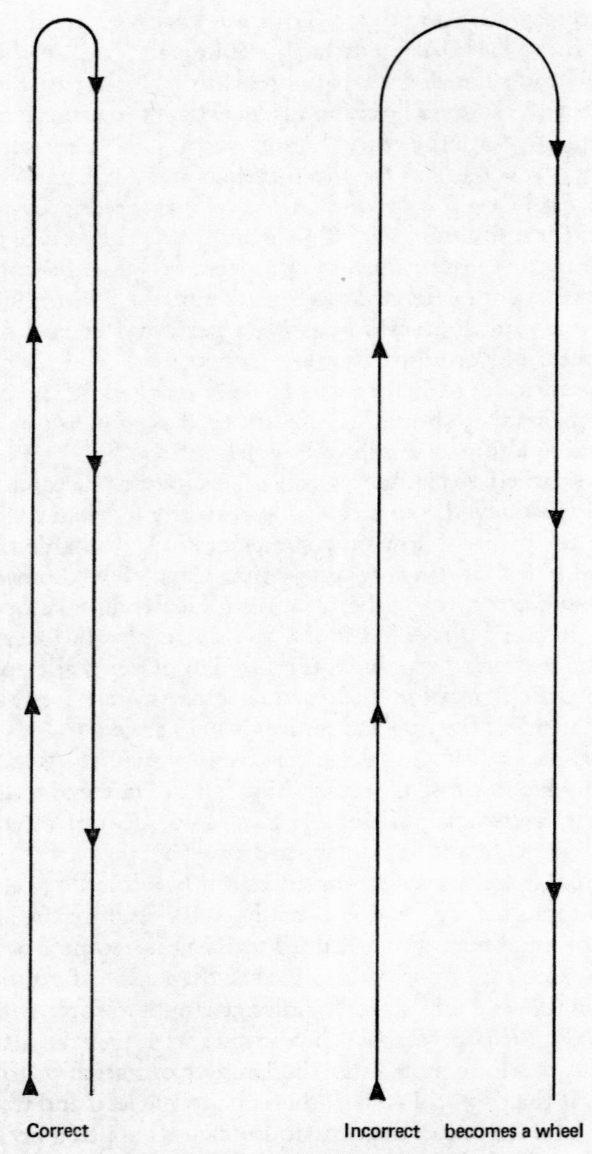

Fig. 1 Heelwork: the about turn

resistance. This is the time to continue with the lesson, but only for two or three minutes and without halting. Remember to stop and play before he becomes bored and do not introduce the halts yet.

It is preferable to perfect straight lines with the dog at the normal fast and slow pace before any turns or halts are introduced, retaining his attention at all times. Gradually the handler can introduce right turns, then about turns, and finally left turns. In all instances starting from the first attempt, the turns should be executed as a definite turn and not a wheel. If the handler firss teaches the dog turns by wheeling this will encourage wide turnt which are far more difficult to correct later than if they were not allowed to develop in the first place (see Figure 1).

The halts can be taught as a separate exercise, avoiding the association of being manhandled into the sit position with the heelwork. Keep the heelwork training moving and flowing, and having broken up the training session by playing and practising other exercises, clip the lead on again and practise several halts over a few yards. To do this the lead should be transferred from the left to the right hand, leaving the left hand free to place on the dog's hindquarters to obtain the *straight sit*. The right hand controls the front of the dog by holding the lead tight above his head. Whilst this manoeuvre is carried out the command 'Sit' should be given, followed by praise immediately the dog responds. Until the handler is certain of a straight sit this procedure should be used every time. For instance, the handler has achieved much more by insisting on quick straight sits on say three occasions by using the described training aids, than if he chances ten halts without the aids and on one halt the dog sits slowly or in an incorrect position.

It can be argued that by teaching the dog to pay attention during heelwork training it detracts from his ability to take note of what is going on in the vicinity. Personally I have never found this to be the case, for a dog has a far wider field of vision than a human and it is a very stupid dog that will ignore potential danger to himself or his handler. Instinct for these things will overcome obedience training.

It will be noted that until now no mention has been made of *heelfree*. My reason for this is that heelfree cannot be taught. Heelwork is perfected on the lead and only when this stage is reached should heelfree be attempted, using the left hand and the voice as encouragement. At the first sign of any fault, revert to heel on lead. It is as simple as that. Remember to keep heelwork lessons confined to just a few minutes, playing with the dog for a greater part of the time in between.

Do not forget to encourage whenever necessary and always to *praise* when response is forthcoming. Remember that over-use of the lead will not keep a dog happy. Always keep halts to a minimum, and when halted the dog must always sit correctly, avoiding continual correction and consequent apprehension. Remember to make heelwork fun for the dog.

Some readers may possess an adult dog that they wish to train for heelwork, or a dog that is somewhat untidy on this exercise. Whilst many of the principles described before can be applied a certain amount of correction may be unavoidable. The reader is however advised to obtain the maximum effect with the minimum amount of correction and thus obtain a happy heelworker.

THE RETRIEVE

For a potential Working Trial dog, the retrieve is without doubt the most important of all the basic exercises. Tracking and searching are just extensions of the retrieve, and nosework accounts for the majority of the allocated marks in most stakes. If competition is seriously contemplated the retrieve exercise must be mastered in such a way that the end result is a dog happily retrieving under complete control.

It was stated in the first chapter that it is necessary to look for a strong retrieve instinct when purchasing a puppy. This cannot be over-stressed, for whilst it is possible to teach a dog the retrieve when there is little or no instinct for it, such a dog is unlikely to search willingly or track. At the same time a dog that retrieves naturally must be taught the exercises for if he only retrieves to please himself, the day will come in competition when he does not wish to retrieve, and there will be nothing the handler can do about it.

As we have dealt with the puppy as well as the mature dog, it must be remembered that on no account should a puppy be scolded for picking up any of the many articles he will have access to in the home. It is only the basic retrieve instinct which makes the puppy pick up a slipper. Do not scold him but rather take it out of his mouth *praising* him as you do so. It is far better to remove the objects to which he has access and give him his own toys than to correct him and risk killing his retrieve instinct.

I prefer to teach the dog to pick up and hold an article on command even if that dog will already run out, pick up, return and deliver to hand naturally. Once taught, the hold command can always be used to advantage, no matter what retrieve exercise is being performed. To do this it is preferable to have the dog on the lead tied to a post or the lead securely held under the foot. This allows the handler freedom of both hands and the dog cannot run off should he not wish to co-operate. Take the dumb-bell in one hand and with the other hand compel the dog to open his jaws by pressing the loose skin gently against the teeth of the lower jaw. Simultaneously give the command 'Hold' and as the dog's mouth opens, place the dumb-bell in his mouth. Immediately place the left hand under the dog's lower jaw in such a manner that will make it impossible for him to eject the dumb-bell, and use the right hand to soothe and stroke him, *praising* whilst the command is repeated in a firm quiet manner. The dog should only be expected to hold for a few seconds at this stage, the handler giving the further command 'Leave' as the dumb-bell is taken out of the dog's mouth. This should be repeated until the dog does not try to eject the dumb-bell and the left hand can be moved a few inches away from the lower jaw. Should the dog attempt to eject the dumb-bell, the left hand is quickly replaced under the lower jaw making it impossible for him to do so. Each time the command 'Hold' is given the dumb-bell should be held in front of the dog's nose allowing him the chance of taking it without being compelled to do so. It may well be that the first sign of success is that on command the dog will slightly open his jaws and whilst it is still necessary to place the dumb-bell in his mouth, *praise* should be given to encourage him.

The next stage is where on command the dog will visibly move his head towards the dumb-bell and take it himself, and once again *praise* should not be forgotten. Ninety per cent of the battle is now over and a controlled retrieve is not far away.

From now on the dumb-bell should be held further away from the dog, progressively lower, but it should be possible for him to grasp it without having to move his feet. Should a dog refuse even though he has previously taken the dumb-bell, it should be placed in his mouth by the method described above and the handler should not keep repeating the command 'Hold' unless action is taken to see that the dog does so. As a rule of thumb guide, if there was no response to the first command, the second time the command is given a dog should be compelled to take it.

Eventually the handler will be able to place the dumb-bell on the ground just in front of the dog, holding one side of it by the hand, and on command the dog will bend forward and take hold of it. So far so good, but there is still one more slightly tricky stage to overcome. That is when the dumb-bell is placed on the ground in front of the dog without the handler's hand on the end of it. It will quickly be seen that once a dog cannot see the hand on the dumb-bell he is inclined to think that he cannot be compelled. If this should be so, on the second command force him to accept it and continue to do so until the hand is unnecessary and the dog will pick up the dumb-bell of his own accord and without the hand on it. Once a dog will do this a retrieve is possible, but start by placing the dumb-bell just a few feet in front of him and give the command 'Hold'. When he picks it up and has it securely in his mouth, call his name in an urgent manner and say 'Fetch', encouraging the dog into the present position by drawing the hand towards the groin thus giving the same hand signal as he has been taught for the recall.

It cannot be emphasized enough that the dog must have been taught to sit straight during recall training to avoid any correction of sits while in the 'present' position, otherwise he could associate such correction with the retrieve which will mean apprehension of the exercise. This is likely to cause a slow unwilling retrieve which is to be avoided at all costs. The time to get the present correct is during recall training and it should be automatic by the time the retrieve is taught.

If all has gone well up to this point, the dog can be sat in the heel position, given the command to 'sit' (not stay), the dumb-bell thrown and the command 'Fetch' given. For a speedy return, continue to call the dog's name once in an urgent manner when he has picked up. The schedule for the test of the retrieve states that the exercise should be executed at a smart pace or gallop, and if the handler has a dog with a strong retrieve instinct which has been preserved throughout training, then a fast happy return will be evident. If however, the dog is somewhat slow or hesitant to retrieve, dispense with the sit at heel, letting the dog run out whilst the dumb-bell is thrown, throwing again once the dog has presented himself with the dumb-bell, and using a lot of urgent encouragement and *praise*.

Once the dog has been taught a controlled retrieve with a dumb-bell as required in competition, he should over a period of time be taught to retrieve strange articles such as will be found in the search and track exercise. It is quite amazing how many handlers overlook this part of the dog's training. Many dogs locate the articles in the search exercise and then refuse to pick them up. It would be quite impossible to state the many types of articles that a judge is likely to provide, but a visit to one or two trials will soon give the reader an idea of what can be encountered. The handler should not attempt to start a dog on the most difficult types of article as soon as the dumb-bell retrieve has been mastered but gradually progress to the difficult articles as the easy objects are successfully retrieved and the dog gains confidence.

Chewing the article, or 'mouthing' as it is known, is a difficult problem to cure. The best way to avoid it is not to let the fault develop in the first place. When retrieve training first commences, any sign of mouthing must be stopped immediately otherwise it will persist throughout the dog's working life. If the dog attempts to mouth the dumb-bell or any other article, with the hand tap him under the jaw, simultaneously scolding using a firm tone of voice. Immediately he ceases to mouth *praise* in a pleasing tone, but revert to scolding at any further sign of mouthing. If the handler does not allow the fault to develop then all is well, but it is extremely difficult to cure a dog of mouthing if this fault has been allowed to develop for any length of time.

THE FINISH

Going from the 'present' position to the 'heel' position is commonly known as the 'finish', and although this is usually regarded as part of the recall or retrieve exercise, there is good reason for dealing with it separately. The finish should be treated as a separate exercise to avoid problems which arise if the finish is always practised after the present. Dogs are creatures of habit and very soon learn what to expect next unless steps are taken to keep them guessing. For example, the finish that is always practised after a present can mean that the handler ends up with a dog which constantly anticipates the command to do so, or sits crooked at an angle which will make his first movement for the finish easier. To avoid this the handler should teach the exercise entirely divorced from either the recall or retrieve, and even when all these exercises have been perfected the finish should only occasionally follow the present during training. It is purely a matter of choice whether the handler decides to use a right- or left-hand finish and either method is acceptable in competition. I generally teach a dog to finish the way that he accepts most readily, therefore advice will be offered to cover either way and the handler can try both to see which method suits the dog.

The basic method of teaching the right-hand finish is to start with the dog sitting at the 'present' position, and in view of the foregoing remarks, rather than calling the dog into the present, just tell him to sit and then stand in front of him. Take the lead in the right hand allowing only an inch or two of slack when the right arm is held at the handler's side. Give the command 'Heel' and as this is done, give the lead a firm jerk simultaneously moving the right arm back in line with the right leg which should be moved one step back. As the dog moves, keep the lead tight so that he is guided to a position slightly behind the right-hand side of the body. When he reaches this position the lead should be transferred behind the handler's back from the right to the left hand, and the right foot should be simultaneously replaced to its original position as the dog is now guided into the heel position. At the last moment the lead is passed back to the right hand leaving the left hand free to be placed on the dog's hindquarters thus pressing him into a perfectly *straight* sit. Again the reader will notice that *straight* has been emphasized and there should really be no question of anything else. The handler has the voice, the lead and the hand, and a combination of all three correctly applied will ensure that the dog is in the exact position required each and every time the exercise is practised.

When the finish has been perfected on the lead and the dog moves on command fractionally before the jerk of the lead, the handler can try without lead assistance, remembering to give the same hand movement as this will now be the signal for the finish, so that voice or signal, or both, can be used in future. There are several variations of this method. For example, starting with the dog in the present, the handler can move to a starting position so that the right leg is level with the right side of the dog's face. It will be seen that this makes the initial movement easier for the dog as he now has less to do to complete the finish. The lead is passed behind the thighs of the handler and held in the left hand, and on the command 'Heel' is tightened, thus drawing the dog around behind the handler to the heel position. With this variation the right leg can still be moved back in such a way that it has the effect of tightening the lead and therefore moving the dog.

The left-hand finish can be accomplished in a similar fashion by taking a pace back with the left leg. Whilst the handle of the lead is held in the right hand, the left hand traverses along the lead from the handle to the slip chain making an outward circling motion so the dog is guided round into the heel position.

The vigilant reader will no doubt have noticed my deliberate error and that is of course that at no time in the section have I mentioned the word 'praise'. When a dog responds to any training *praise* is always a must.

THE SENDAWAY

As a name for an exercise 'the sendaway' is descriptive for in competition the handler is required by the judge to send the dog away to a pre-determined place. It is widely argued that it has the least practical value of all the scheduled tests but from a spectator's point of view it is interesting to watch. This is probably because the ability to control a dog at a distance is more impressive than control with the dog in close proximity to the handler. The exercise does have practical uses when a dog is required to search and quarter an area for a criminal or missing person as in the Police Dog Stake.

To teach a dog to go away on command is relatively simple. The difficulty arises with teaching a dog to go to the exact place required, which, though being obvious to the handler, is far from obvious to a dog. With all training confusion should be avoided, and with this exercise there are many opportunities for this to arise. For instance, if the handler cannot drop or stop his dog instantly, at a distance, on one command, it is pointless to attempt to teach the sendaway. If the dog has been accurately sent to the required place and then wanders whilst the handler continually shouts the command, the dog may confuse such shouting with having gone to the wrong place.

In Chapter 1 the description of a puppy sendaway to food did not include dropping the puppy, therefore these remarks should not be construed as contradictory. The puppy sendaway is only a means of association of the request 'Away' with happily leaving the handler rather than leaving under duress. Assuming that the puppy has been taught to go away to his food and the time has come for him to learn the exercise properly, all that is necessary is to take his feeding dish out into the garden with a tit-bit in it. Place it at the end of the garden in an obvious place. Do not attempt a long sendaway at first but rather take him to approximately ten or twelve yards away and sit the dog in the heel position. Place the hands either side of his face so that they act as blinkers and cut down his angle of vision thus only the immediate area of his feeding dish is visible. Be very gentle with the hands and do not maul the dog around for this aid is merely to assist him to focus in a particular direction. Whilst focussing his eyes it is helpful to repeat quietly the command 'Away' or use separate words such as 'Look straight', and if the same procedure is always adopted the dog will soon learn he is about to be sent and that he should focus in the direction the handler is indicating. When ready, stand up straight and if necessary give the dog a command to sit still, and after one or two seconds' pause the command should be given in a quiet pleasant manner. As soon as the dog reaches his dish let him eat the tit-bit and then give the command 'Down'. Should the dog take the wrong direction at this or any subsequent stage, do not attempt re-direction or continual commands, but call him back and start again. This time give him the command to sit and go and stand behind the dish. Call the dog to you, and when he has eaten the tit-bit, give the command 'Down'. Once the dog is happily going to his dish the distance can gradually be increased and the tit-bit occasionally left out until it is possible to send him to the dish without the use of food. It must be stressed that the use of food must be kept to a minimum otherwise it is possible the dog will only work for food. The handler should not attempt to move the sendaway area further on when increasing distance, but should move back from the original starting place to increase distance. The reason for this is that the dog would want to stop at the place he was sent to previously, but by starting further back the dog is sent to the same place each time and much confusion is avoided.

As soon as the food has been dispensed with, some mark other than his dish should be used, such as a pole. The only reason the marker is used is for teaching the dog to focus, and the type of marker should be changed regularly. Rarely does a judge set his sendaway with an obvious marker. Sometimes it is used in the lower stakes, but rarely in TD or PD. It is more likely that the judge will select a particular patch of grass, a distant tree or a hole in a fence, etc. In other words a judge will go out of his way to select a place which can easily be described to the handler but is not at all obvious to the dog. This is where the sendaway at Obedience Shows differs from the Trials sendaway, making the latter much more difficult, and rightly so.

The end product of teaching the dog to look towards the marker is to be able to set the dog up and focus his eyes in the direction required. It should be remembered that the dog should be sitting straight and not at an angle to the direction of the sendaway, so that his back is also in line with the direction in which he is being sent.

Once the dog has been perfected over short distances in the garden it is necessary to build up distances of up to 200 yards. It is unlikely that a dog will be required to go more than 200 yards in competition, but on the other hand it is just as unlikely that a judge will set less than 100 yards in the higher stakes. This is done on the same principle of using the same place in which the dog is dropped and moving the starting point further away. An ideal time to do this is whilst exercising the dog in the country. Whenever there is a long straight path the dog can be dropped whilst the handler walks on. When satisfied with the distance the handler can call the dog and then *send* him back to the place in which he was previously dropped. Whilst the dog is going away the handler can quietly walk backwards building up further distance, and then repeat the procedure. The dog must gain absolute confidence in going away over a long distance, therefore whilst training for distance it is preferable for the path to have natural obstacles on either side, making it impossible for the dog to go in the wrong direction and therefore avoiding confusion in his mind.

I am a great believer in endeavouring never to allow a dog to go wrong in training. Every time the dog performs any exercise correctly in training then progress has been made no matter how many aids were used to achieve that perfection. Conversely each time the dog goes wrong the handler is only building up confusion in the dog's mind and this should be avoided at all costs. Therefore when practising the sendaway, unless reasonably confident of a perfect sendaway with one command, I prefer to recall the dog to the place where I have decided to send him, dropping him on arrival rather than using the normal recall present, then attempting the sendaway to the same place. Should the dog have travelled two or three yards in what is obviously the wrong direction, rather than let him continue in this direction or give further commands, I call him back to me and go through the recall procedure before sending him to the designated spot. It should be remembered that a dog will always want to return to the spot he has been to before and this is the reason for the recall. It makes it easier for the dog to understand where he is being sent. For the same reason never attempt to send a dog to the correct place if he has just previously gone in the wrong direction, for he will most likely repeat his mistake unless prior action such as a recall is taken to put him right. Likewise in training, the handler should not keep changing the direction of the sendaway in the same session, for again the dog will invariably want to return to a place where he has previously been sent. If the handler wishes to give the dog a different sendaway the area should be large enough for each attempt to be at a different place.

Should the reader wish to teach an adult dog that has not had any previous sendaway training, then commence with recalls with a down at the end as described earlier, or in the case of a very awkward dog, run him out to the designated spot on a loose lead giving the command 'Away' as the run commences. In the past this method has been much favoured by handlers but it should be remembered that it involves compulsion, whereas all that has been said in this section so far does not involve compulsion at all, just careful painstaking teaching. The likely trouble with compulsion is apprehension, except with a tough dog, and this type is in the minority.

RE-DIRECTION

Both the TD and PD Stakes require the dog to be re-directed at the end of a sendaway, but training for re-direction should not be introduced until the dog is proficient and confident at long distance sendaways. One of the quickest ways to ruin a good sendaway is to practise re-direction at the end of it. The two should only be married together in competition, or in training with a very experienced dog. The handler who makes this mistake may well wonder why the dog is frequently going away from him in anything but the right direction and then waiting for a further command to the right place. The reason being that the dog has become so used to being re-directed prior to perfecting the sendaway that his association of ideas is that the handler will eventually direct him to the required place and anywhere will do initially.

It must be remembered that in competition this exercise will have to be performed at great distances. It is therefore wise to use a command and a signal when training commences, and used simultaneously both are acceptable in competition. The obvious commands are 'Right' and 'Left' combined with an arm signal.

The handler should never attempt to practise both left and right until the dog is well advanced for this will cause confusion. One way should be practised until the handler is capable of re-directing the dog that way from a good distance. When this is so the opposite direction can be practised.

It should also be obvious to the reader that as with the sendaway itself, training of this nature should not be attempted until the handler is capable of stopping the dog in either the stand, sit, or down at a distance, on one command. It is difficult enough to teach re-direction without the added confusion of trying to stop the dog when it reaches the required place.

To start re-direction training a field with a long wire fence is an ideal location. The dog should be on one side of the fence and the handler on the other. This fence will stop the dog making ground towards the handler which is his natural inclination, until certain of what is required. There should only be a matter of two or three yards between the handler and the dog who should be stationary. The handler should give the command and signal, and run along the fence encouraging the dog to do likewise on the other side. A reasonable distance should be covered before the dog is stopped and praised lavishly to ensure that apprehension does not set in. The dog can now be taken back to the starting point and the exercise repeated. This can be done four or five times during that session before training ceases. As the dog gains in confidence the handler should gradually stop running with him until he is able to stand still and re-direct the dog the one way without there being any distance between dog and handler at the starting point. It will also be necessary to stop the dog and then send him on again in the same direction so that he does not associate the second command as being the end of the exercise, but care should be taken to ensure that the dog covers the maximum distance during the first re-direction of each training session. If the handler continually sends the dog a short distance initially, and subsequently tries to send the dog past the previous point at which he has been stopped, the dog is less likely to want to proceed past this point than he would, had the maximum distance been used first, followed by shorter distances.

As the dog gains in confidence the handler can move back from the fence, a few yards at a time, thus leaving the dog to travel his same path. The fence between dog and handler has even more importance now for it will stop the dog's natural reaction of trying to re-direct at an angle so that he is able to pass close to the handler as he has been taught to do when the handler was close to the fence. Once the handler has moved back from the fence, each time he has sent the dog to the extremity in one direction it will be necessary for him to return to the dog, praise him, and then playfully take him back to the starting point for further practice in the same direction. This will entail a lot of walking and there is a great temptation to try and re-direct the opposite way to save the handler having continually to rejoin his dog and take the dog back to the start. The handler should avoid this temptation, for a dog who has been taught perfect re-direction one way before being trained for the opposite way will, in the long run, be the more reliable. Once either left or right-hand re-direction has been perfected, then the opposite direction should be trained for by starting from the beginning again. It will probably take several training sessions to perfect the dog in one direction, and many before the handler can safely re-direct from a distance in both directions. Each time a fresh training session commences it is wise for the handler to start at a closer distance to the dog than that at which he finished the previous session. When the dog is proficient at both directions at long distances, a fresh training location can be used with a fence once again having the effect of keeping the dog from coming back at an angle towards the handler. When the dog is successfully working behind a fence on various locations, then he can be tried in a field without a fence, but any attempt to come back towards the handler must be corrected immediately before it becomes a habit.

It must be stressed again that if the dog lacks in confidence on the sendaway and re-direction is introduced, confusion in the dog's mind will result and it will be the handler's fault and not the dog's. Also I stress again, the sendaway and re-direction should only be married together in competition and not in training until the dog is very experienced.

SPEAK AND CEASE SPEAKING

In this exercise the dog is required to bark on command and to cease barking immediately on further command. It is practical for the police and civilian dog as an undoubted deterrent when handler and dog are faced with people whose intentions are not desirable. Occasionally a judge will set this test with the dog out of sight of his handler, therefore it is necessary for the dog to speak on a vocal command without visual signals. On the other hand, as a practical exercise it is useful for the dog to respond to a signal which is not obvious to anyone the handler wishes the dog to threaten.

Before attempting to teach the dog this exercise, observe him over a period of time and take note of what motivates him to bark naturally. Select the most suitable motivation and as he barks give the command 'Speak' followed by praise. Keep repeating the command with praise but cease immediately the dog stops barking. This must be repeated over a period of time until the dog will respond to the command without motivation. At this stage, if required a signal can also be introduced and both command and signal should be given until the dog responds to either. It may also be necessary to introduce a command such as 'Quiet' so that the dog will cease barking on command. The aim should be to train the dog to *speak* without cessation on one command until ordered by his handler to stop.

With a greedy type of dog food can be used to induce barking, but care should be exercised and the food omitted as soon as possible as this could result in having a dog that will only speak when food is offered.

There are a few dogs who are loath to give tongue, and here artificial means of inducement may be necessary. One of the most successful methods I have come across is to take the dog to unfamiliar isolated surroundings and tie him to whatever happens to be convenient. The handler should then stride away in a purposeful manner giving the impression he is leaving his dog and does not intend to return. Whilst the handler is walking away the dog can be repeatedly called in an excited manner, and as he is tied and unable to get to the handler he may well give tongue. As soon as the dog starts to bark then the previously described procedure can be adopted, which at first will be at a distance. It should be realized that as the handler returns and gets progressively nearer the dog his feelings of isolation will diminish, so it may be necessary to turn away again to ensure continual barking. Perhaps I should introduce a word of caution here for I adopted this method with one of my dogs who had hardly ever barked. Having taught him to bark, at the next trial he was entered at I found my dog had decided that all that was necessary to recall his handler was to sit and bark during the down stay, expecting me to return and praise him for barking. The down stay was the remaining exercise and until then my dog was in the lead. Needless to say he did not even qualify that day! Following this episode several weeks of patient re-training of the stay was necessary before he realized he could not call me back whenever he wished. A good friend of mine has the very apt description of 'handler's recall' for this behaviour. A lesson was learned the hard way, for whilst teaching my dog something I required, I inadvertently taught him something undesirable.

STEADINESS TO GUNSHOT

In the first chapter, mention was made of allowing the puppy to be gradually introduced to sudden noises, and if this procedure is followed it is quite a simple transition to actual gunfire.

When commencing training the handler will require an assistant to fire the gun, for both the handler and the dog should be at a distance of at least 100 yards whilst gunfire is introduced. The object is to assure the dog that the sudden crack of a gun does not signal danger to him and cause consequent apprehension.

The dog should be praised and stroked whilst the gun is fired, and both trainer and dog should move progressively nearer to the gun all the time the dog is not showing the slightest sign of fear. Should fear become evident, then stay at the same distance and play with the dog whilst the gun is fired until he realizes that no harm will befall him.

Should the dog be a keen retriever then articles can be thrown in play to keep the dog happy during the gunfire.

Any sign of excited barking or lack of control that could result in the dog eventually attacking on the sound of gunfire should be stopped right at the beginning. Proceed with caution and do not overdo the gunfire during the early sessions, but rather build up the dog's confidence over a period of time until he is quite happy with a ·45 being fired within a few feet of him.

3

Agility

GENERAL

At Working Trials the competing dogs are required to negotiate three different types of jump. There is a maximum of twenty marks, fourteen of these marks being the minimum to qualify a dog in this group.

The jumps are often the source of worry to the beginner, and indeed some of the more experienced handlers worry over these exercises. More dogs are prematurely retired from trials because for reasons of age they are no longer fit to jump than for any other reason, many of these same dogs still being capable of first-class performances in other tests.

Handlers should always be certain that their dogs are fit enough to be taught to jump. For example, it is unfair to ask a grossly overweight dog to jump, but far worse is jumping a dog with a bad case of hip dysplasia, and owners of breeds subject to this complaint would do well to seek veterinary advice before attemptin to teach jumping. Likewise, a puppy should not be taught to jump until his bones have matured for much damage can be done. As a rule of thumb, the dog should be fourteen to fifteen months old before any form of serious jumping is attempted, the most dangerous part of jumping being the landing, particularly with the scale jump.

The agility tests have great practical value and whilst for convenience I am a believer in teaching a dog by using the same type of jumps to be found at trials, once the dog has mastered these jumps a wise handler will introduce ditches and streams for practical long jumps, walls and fences for scale jumps, and smaller obstacles for clear jumps. This introduces the practical side to the dog and will also be of value to the handler who can never be quite sure of the type of jumps that the society promoting the trial will provide.

One of the mistakes the beginner makes is to teach his dog to jump quite soundly over his own jumps in his own garden and he is then mystified when the dog refuses to jump at the first trial at which he is entered. The reason is quite simple, for the dog is suddenly confronted with a strange set of jumps in a different environment, and far from being disobedient by refusing to jump, he just doesn't yet understand that the command to jump applies to anything other than his own set of equipment in his own garden. The wise handler, having taught the dog to master his own jumps, will therefore arrange to use other people's in different environments before his dog is entered at a trial.

This chapter on jumping has deliberately been set after training for control, for a dog should not be taught to jump until the handler has complete control of the dog. In the Companion Dog Stake handlers can very often be seen with dogs that need to be held back with the collar for fear that they will jump prematurely, or they are unable to control the dog on the other side of the jump. The experienced judge will penalize this, and rightly so, for nothing looks worse to a spectator than handlers whose dogs do not appear to be under control. I never teach a dog to jump until I have a perfect immediate down and can approach any jump with the dog at heelfree without touching him. Apart from looking untidy in competition, it is obvious that a dog which continually needs correction for such faults in training can become confused as to whether the correction is for jumping or for lack of control.

For the purpose of distinction between jumping for distance in the long jump and jumping for height in the clear and scale jump, two separate commands are helpful. At Working Trials the three jumps are usually in close proximity. The two commands help the inexperienced dog to avoid confusion as to which obstacle he is required to go over.

The agility exercises are the factor which limits the smaller dog from qualifying beyond the Utility Dog Stakes. Whilst the rules allow the jumps to be contracted and lowered for small dogs up to and including this stake, any dog that exceeds fifteen inches in height at the shoulder has to negotiate the full length and heights to qualify beyond UD.

During any prolonged period of inactivity on the scale jump, it is a good idea to put the dog over the clear jump on several occasions each week. This helps to keep the jumping muscles in trim.

THE CLEAR JUMP

Working Trials required heights

Dogs not exceeding 10 inches at shoulder	1 foot 6 inches
Dogs not exceeding 15 inches at shoulder	2 feet
Dogs exceeding 15 inches at shoulder	3 feet

It is normal practice to teach a dog to clear jump the required height on command before progressing to the scale jump. Commence the dog's lessons with the top bar six to nine inches high from the ground, and with the dog on a long slack lead, give the command 'Up' guiding the dog over the bar as you do so, remembering to *praise* him as he lands. If necessary, to give him confidence the handler can step over the jump with the dog. A little bribery is quite permissible with the right type of dog. For instance, a favourite toy placed at the other side of the jump is an incentive to the retrieve-happy dog, and if the handler allows him to pick it up when he has negotiated the jump, it also acts as a reward and makes jumping a happy game. Keep repeating this manoeuvre until you are certain that the lead can be dispensed with and the dog will happily jump over the low bar without a lead. This is the time to raise the bar, but only approximately three inches at a time, and at each stage the dog should jump perfectly under control before asking him for increased height. Once the height is such that it is possible for the dog to go under rather than over, a second or third bar may be necessary to fill the gap beneath, but when the dog can jump two-thirds of the required height, it is advisable to dispense with the lower bars occasionally so that he will jump on command even though it is quite possible for him to run underneath. Providing the handler does not rush matters and over a period of time ensures that the dog is happy at each height, eventually the dog will jump the maximum height required for his size without the space beneath the top bar being filled. It is however advisable with all three jumps to perfect the dog over five per cent greater height or length in practice to ensure that he can happily negotiate the maximum height at trials.

The handler can now add the control on the far side of the jump by introducing the immediate down which should have been perfected long before jumping commenced. A sit or stand is also acceptable, control being the important point.

THE SCALE JUMP

Working Trials required heights

Dogs not exceeding 10 inches at shoulder	3 feet
Dogs not exceeding 15 inches at shoulder	4 feet
Dogs exceeding 15 inches at shoulder	6 feet

Having perfected the clear jump the dog can now be introduced to the scale jump at the maximum height that he has successfully traversed with the clear jump. Allow him to gain confidence on this new jump by allowing him to clear it before attempting to raise it. If the boards are six inches deep, once the dog is happily clearing the height he is used to, insert another board and again allow time for confidence to build up, assuming that he still clears the new height. Additional boards can be inserted until such time as the dog commences to scale of his own accord or refuses to jump because he feels he is unable to clear it. Put the dog on the lead again if the latter is the case and gently assist him to jump on to the top and down the other side by passing the lead over the scale and running beside it as the dog jumps. Continue to add boards until it becomes necessary for him to scale by obtaining leverage with his front paws on the top board whilst his back paws scramble at the lower ones.

At this stage, or before, it is advisable to start the dog from both sides of the jump and then to leave him sitting on one side with the lead draped over the top board. The handler should go to the far side and give the command 'Up', slapping the top board with the hand and keeping slight tension on the lead as the dog jumps. The handler must remember to back off as the dog reaches the top to allow him room to land, and as he does so he should adopt the stance used for the present of the recall with the two hands coming into the groin which is the signal the dog has been taught for a present. Here again we have another example of how new lessons are made much easier for both dog and handler if the basic exercises have been carefully observed. One such example was the use of the immediate down on the far side of the clear jump, and now the already perfected present when training for the recall over the scale.

The handler should continue to add new boards gradually and it will probably be found easier to control the lead if the dog jumps from one side, with the handler on the other side. If possible, as each new board is happily negotiated by the dog, take the lead off and allow him to jump without it. When I first dispense with a lead, although I unclip it from his collar I still drape it over the scale and pull it towards me as the dog jumps. In this way he thinks he is still attached to it, but this practice is only necessary on the first two or three attempts and acts as a transition from scaling on the lead to scaling without lead assistance. It is wise to revert to the attached lead each time a new board is added, thus making it less likely that the dog will refuse.

Whilst the scale jump is low enough for the handler to see what the dog is doing when he lands on the far side without lead assistance, a decision must now be made as to whether the dog is going to be left in the stand, sit or down position, for at a Working Trial the judge will ask you to nominate one of those three positions and the dog is expected to adopt that position prior to the steward telling you to recall the dog over the jump. The handler must also have noted the dog's ideal take-off distance from the jump, and if necessary send the dog on until he reaches that position.

Whilst no two dogs of any breed necessarily jump the same way, most Alsatians seem to prefer to start from quite close to the jump whereas Border Collies usually like to start further back. It is up to the handler to realize the distance from the scale his particular dog is best suited to, both for sending over and recalling.

I feel it is immaterial in which position the dog is left at the far side of the jump, and my advice would be for the handler to choose the position that the dog can be guaranteed to adopt on command, for 20 per cent of the marks for the scale jump are allotted to the dog remaining steady before being recalled. To recapitulate and punctuate this section a few Dos and Donts are appended.

The Dos

1 Keep the dog happy at all times and make it a game.
2 Praise the dog every time he responds, and always remember the praise and the friendly pat throughout his jumping life.
3 Put a lot of enthusiasm and encouragement into the commands.
4 Progress slowly if necessary over many weeks.
5 Ensure your scale jump is rigid when the dog jumps or else he may mistrust it.
6 Revert to the previous height when and if the dog objects to an increase in height.
7 Ensure he is physically fit enough to jump.

The Donts

1 Don't over-tax the dog's strength in any one session.
2 Don't bore him.
3 Don't start jumping lessons until you have control of the dog sitting at heel and adopting the stand, sit or down at a distance.
4 Don't let your lead become entangled with the jump.
5 Don't string the dog up in attempting a height for which he is not yet ready.
6 Don't ask him to do anything of which he is not physically capable by reason of his size.

THE LONG JUMP

Working Trials required heights

Dogs not exceeding 10 inches at shoulder	4 feet
Dogs not exceeding 15 inches at shoulder	6 feet
Dogs exceeding 15 inches at shoulder	9 feet

This is probably the agility exercise the handler will have the most difficulty in teaching, for not only has the dog to gauge the length but also the height of the back boards. It is normal practice for a long jump to be five or six slats, increasing in height from front to back, set at an angle so that from the dog's height the boards look like one continuous expanse of obstacle.

To commence lessons, use two or three boards close together so that they represent a length of two or three feet at the most. Put the dog on a slack long lead and sit him at heel at a reasonable distance from the jump. Give him the command 'Over' and run towards the boards with him. When he reaches them give the command again, and whilst you run along the right hand-side of the jump, tighten the lead just sufficiently to encourage him to clear the boards, but slacken it again as he takes off so that he is not restricted in the air. As he lands make a fuss of him and give plenty of *praise*. As with the scale jump, the handler should allow the dog to gain his confidence at each length before increasing the distance and adding new boards. Do not allow the dog to run through the slats for this habit is difficult to cure. Should the dog attempt to do so, hold the lead that little bit tighter so that it is impossible for him to do so. Long before the dog is capable of jumping the maximum length required it is better to perfect him off the lead on something like half of the required length.

To a beginner the transition from long jumping on the lead to off the lead can seem difficult. The first few times the exercise is attempted without the dog attached to the lead it is a good ruse to quietly unclip it and run with the dog with the lead dangling and, as pointed out with the scale jump, the dog is apt to form the impression that he is still under the controlling influence of the lead, and by the time he realizes this is not so, he is quite happy to jump without lead assistance. As soon as the dog will jump lead free with the handler continuing to run with him past the boards, he should gradually let the dog get ahead of him. At first this will be at the last minute as the dog is airborne, and gradually the handler can drop back at an earlier point until he is able to stop at the first board slightly to the side. Whilst in competition it is permissible for the handler to run with his dog provided that he does not pass the first board, I feel that the handler should continue to drop back at an earlier point until he can confidently send the dog over the jump without moving from the place from which the dog was given the command. This looks more professional in competition than the handler who seemingly has to chase the dog over the obstacle. Once the dog has perfected approximately half the maximum distance it is simply a matter of gradually increasing length, ensuring that he is confident with the existing length before each increase is made.

At first it is quite possible that the dog will frequently clip and therefore knock over the last board, but this is generally only a matter of the dog's inexperience and he will soon learn to time his leap and gain sufficient height to avoid doing so. It cannot be over-stressed that, as with other jumps, the handler should proceed slowly and not overdo it in any one session. Immediately the dog has successfully jumped there is nothing like playing with him or letting him retrieve his favourite article or toy. Reward makes for happy jumping as opposed to apprehension.

4

Nosework

THEORY

There can be no doubt that nosework is the basis of Working Trials. Whilst it is desirable to have a good degree of control before this type of training commences, the reader should be aware that over 50 per cent of the total marks in most stakes are awarded to the nosework groups. We are therefore dealing with the exercises in Trials which the prospective competitor cannot afford to fail if success is to be attained.

The canine during its evolution has used its nose as a method of survival and has therefore developed a keen sense of smell. To survive, man has not needed to rely on smell to the same extent. The olfactory mucous membrane has therefore evolved in a different way between man and dog, leaving the dog with a far greater area than his human master.

All dogs can track, for their ancestors did so to hunt food and to find a prospective mate. The name of the game is to induce the dog to track when we want him to although such a track might be uninteresting to the dog. By care and patience, tracks that we wish the dog to follow, can be made to become interesting.

A track consists of a line of scent which the human would call a smell. This smell might be strong or weak, pleasant or displeasing, but above all else it will be made up of moisture. Without moisture scent cannot be retained, and the strength of that scent will depend upon the time taken for the evaporation of the moisture which carries the scent.

We are all familiar with the sudden shower after a long hot dry spell during the summer. Everything smells fresh, the earth, grass and flowers, but given a further period of dry heat this freshness which is moisture, will gradually disappear altogether. After interior decorating the smell of paint and wallpaper paste lingers for many days, gradually disappearing as the moisture which carries that smell evaporates. Cooking smells remain in the kitchen until the moisture created by the cooking evaporates. These examples will give some idea of how scent is carried and how it disappears, but what is the identity of the scent that we train our dogs to follow?

First of all let us consider the scent a human leaves behind when walking. To what extent the scent of the human body effects the track is debatable, and I feel that the percentage is small compared to the other factors that go towards creating the identity of the track. As we all know the human perspires, and movement such as walking or running increases the perspiration through the pores of the skin, although perspiration of certain parts of the body is continual even without movement. Dry skin and loose hairs can fall to the ground as we walk. The scent of a female completely devoid of artificial perfumes and the like is totally different to that of the male and can help to establish a track identity.

The material from which the track-layer's footwear is constructed will have its own smell, some of this smell will be transferred to the ground by walking or running. Then again, minute particles of the footwear material will be left behind on the track. The clothing the track-layer wears has its distinct smell. Whilst walking, various parts of clothing rub together helping to wear the article, again this will leave minute particles on the track. Each type of cloth has its own odour and added to that odour is the smell of any washing powder, cleaning agent or smell that has been impregnated into the cloth by virtue of occupation, such as baker, miner, painter, etc.

We must now consider the effect that the weight and movement of the track-layer's feet have upon the track, and most experienced trainers agree that to a large extent this is what the dog relies on when following a track. As a track-layer or anyone walks across countryside devoid of vegetation, tiny particles of earth and soil are disturbed. Larger lumps of earth are crushed into smaller particles, stones are moved and the whole ground disturbance releases trapped moisture. Where vegetation is growing, as the feet tread and scuff in the act of walking, that vegetation will be bruised and crushed. This will release moisture and odour, the odour is the agent which will be carried by the moisture, and until that moisture evaporates, the odour will be apparent. This leaves a smell stronger, and somewhat different, from that which surrounds it, but as evaporation progresses the smell will correspondingly decline.

All these factors go towards giving the track an identity of its own, but when the personal scent of the individual is too weak and another track of the same age crosses the one which the dog is following, even an experienced tracking dog can be misled. However part of track identity is the age, for if a dog is following a young track on which evaporation is in its early stages and another much older track in later stages of evaporation crosses it, the experienced dog will know the difference and should not be misled. The same situation in reverse should not pose any undue problems for the experienced dog, as it is the difference in the age of the track which largely creates its identity.

Many people think that time is the all important factor effecting scent. It is not time on its own which destroys the scent, but the exposure to the elements which will cause evaporation. Let us now consider how this exposure to the elements will affect the time of scent retention. The sun at noon on a very hot dry summer's day will cause rapid evaporation, but that same sun, unhindered by clouds in the middle of winter, will not evaporate moisture anywhere near as quickly. So the strength of heat from the sun is of prime importance.

Changes in temperature will also affect evaporation. During the late afternoon and evening the temperature is falling and so is the rate of evaporation. Around dawn the temperature will start to rise from the night temperature level, and with each rise the rate of evaporation increases. Experiment for yourself with a good tracking dog by setting a track pattern and laying one in the morning at 8 a.m. to be worked by the dog four hours later. Then lay the same track pattern on similiar ground at 8 p.m. to be worked twelve hours later. The overnight track will have a lower evaporation rate than the four-hour-old day track, and in all probability the dog will work the former track with less difficulty than the latter track.

In only the most severe weather such as heavy driving rain combined with high wind is the scent completely destroyed

The retrieve, stage 1. Note dog held securely by lead

The retrieve, stage 2. Note dog's head coming towards dumb-bell

Top left. The retrieve, stage 3

Bottom left. The retrieve, stage 4. Note hand still holding the dumb-bell

Right. The retrieve, stage 5. For the first time the dog takes the dumb-bell without the handler's hand on it

Below. The retrieve – the finished product

The right hand finish – first stages

The left hand finish – first stages

Re-direction. Note barrier to keep the dog parallel to the handler

within three hours. Whilst moisture is necessary to retain scent, and indeed a light shower can enhance it, on the other hand continual rain will obliterate the scent in time. The length of that time will depend upon the strength of the rain. Most experienced trialists will be pleased to see dew lying on the ground. How many people realize that dew only forms when the wind is minimal or non-existent so that not only have we additional helpful moisture, but there has been little wind to blow the scent about.

Wind is a factor effecting scent which, when other than light, we can do without. Whilst evaporation destroys scent, strong wind disperses it. Light a garden bonfire on a still day and the smoke will rise in a thick vertical column gradually dispersing some distance above the fire. Light the same bonfire on a day of strong winds and not only is it blown and distributed over a wide area, but that very distribution speeds the dispersal of the smoke. The effect on scent is the same, and whilst a certain amount of wind is helpful for article identification, it does not help the ground scent that we have been discussing so far.

The degree of shelter afforded to a track is another very important factor, for whilst one track may take the full blast of the wind, the track in the field next door may well be shielded by trees and high walls, etc. Such shelter can also affect moisture evaporation on a hot dry day.

Misty conditions are ideal for tracking, for as we know mist is damp and dampness means moisture, and moisture is helpful for scent retention.

Frost and snow can preserve or destroy scent, and this will depend upon whether the track was laid prior to or after the descent of these elements, for a heavy snowfall will bury an existing track.

High humidity is helpful to the tracking dog for this means dampness and moisture again.

Everything we have discussed so far can be described as ground scent, and now we must deal with the scent of the articles left on the track or in the search area, which for the purpose of this book we will describe as wind scent. The articles will all contain an individual scent of their own according to their composition. This scent will often be foreign to the surroundings and as such will help the dog, exceptions being when the judge has, for instance, decided to use a conker for an article and the track or search is laid amongst chestnut trees in the autumn. For our purpose we teach dogs to ignore the individual scent and only indicate those articles which contain human scent. This individual and human scent is borne to the dog on the wind or breeze if apparent, and when so a dog can indicate an article from many yards away. Wind scent will also greatly assist the patrol dog when searching for hidden criminals or missing persons.

Scent theory could take up much more space, but I feel that this book should remain as simple as possible, and therefore only the main points have been covered. There are one or two people in this country who could write a book on this subject alone, having made a lifelong study of it, and their knowledge is of great interest to the experienced but probably confusing to the beginner. There are also thousands of other scent experts who, unfortunately, because they are of the canine variety, can only convey their knowledge in a limited way. Who knows, if they could read they might cry 'rubbish'! Various scientific theories have been disproved with the march of time and maybe the popular beliefs of today will be altered in the light of future additional knowledge.

TRACKING

A dog is a carnivorous animal and as such, in its original wild state, relied on the use of its nose and ability to track prey for a supply of food. Likewise, today the average domestic dog, given half the chance, will without any training whatsoever track down a bitch in season as a prospective mate. It is this ability to use the nose that we adapt to suit our purpose of tracking a human. In the first chapter I stressed that the handler should choose a puppy with a strong retrieve instinct, for not only is such an instinct going to be highly desirable when teaching the search exercise, it is also the best and most natural way to teach a dog to track.

A dog with a strong retrieve instinct will quickly and enthusiastically learn to track as we wish, providing the handler does not confuse him. Tracking could easily be described as a long distance inanimate retrieve. Most experienced handlers will confirm that when an article is thrown in full sight of the dog it will be retrieved at a faster pace than when an article is placed on the ground and is therefore inanimate. An adult dog with little retrieve instinct which has been taught to retrieve, performing it only because he has to, will make a poor, inanimate retriever. In many cases it is still possible to teach such a dog to track with painstaking patience, but a keen retriever is much better material to work with, and one that will quickly bring rewards to the handler if he teaches the dog carefully. Unfortunately it is so often the handler that ruins a good prospective tracker by not being able to read the dog. Pulling the dog off the track when the handler thinks he knows better than the dog, not knowing exactly where the track is, in the initial stages of training is many a beginner's downfall. When one listens to a handler blaming his dog for failure, in the majority of cases he should blame himself for failing to train, read or handle the dog correctly.

A tracking harness and line will be necessary, for Working Trial Rules require the dog to be worked with this equipment. Before taking the dog out for his first tracking lesson, he should first of all have been allowed to run around in his own home environment wearing the harness. This should only be done for the minimum of time necessary to ensure that when having his first few tracking lessons, his concentration is not being broken by the irritation of something unusual on his body. When he becomes a proficient tracker the harness on his body will mean only one thing to him, and this is *track*. In the absence of a harness for the first one or two lessons a plain leather collar could be used, but definitely not a check chain. However, it is advisable to use the right equipment from the start. Initially a tracking line is unnecessary and very often a liability to the beginner handler, for there is an art in line handling which we will deal with later. More easily managed is a lead or a piece of rope between four and six feet in length.

Grazing land is an ideal surface for the initial training, but the handler should ensure that the land he is to use has not been walked upon by humans or animals during the previous twelve hours, for at this stage crosstracks are undesirable.

If it is possible to take an assistant, preferably one with a sound knowledge of tracking, then so much the better. Whilst the handler holds the dog on his harness and lead, the assistant (the tracklayer) should obtain the dog's interest in a favourite toy by gently teasing the dog to arouse enthusiasm. Having done so, a stake should be placed in the ground and an area of grass, approximately one foot in diameter, should be trodden down around the stake. The track-layer should then walk away from the stake for about twenty-five yards using short heavy paces, then turn to face the dog. His interest in the article should be renewed by waving it and making any necessary noises to attract the dog's attention. The article is then laid on the ground, the track-layer first ensuring that the dog saw the article placed before continuing for several paces more in the same direction. He should then return in a semi-circular route until passing level and at least twenty-five yards away from the starting stake, without returning at all near to it. If the dog accepts this method and at the first attempt goes forward to retrieve the article, occasionally putting his nose to the ground, so well and good. Should the dog lose interest in the article by the distraction of the assistant returning in a different direction, it may be advantageous to change the strategy. If this is the case, once the assistant has reached the end of the twenty-five yards and re-kindled the dog's interest in the article, he should return as quickly as possible over the exact route on which the track was laid.

In either case the handler should then take the dog to the stake, encourage him to put his nose down to the well-trodden area around the stake, and briefly inhale the scent. Whilst doing so, the dog should be given the command 'Track' in a soothing manner. If the dog is a keen retriever he will immediately start to work the track. To give the dog an idea of what is required, the first few tracks should be laid into the wind, but only until such time as the dog understands that he should track. The handler should take care to ensure that the dog stays on the line of the track by gentle use of the lead. When the dog is on track he can occasionally quietly encourage him, but this should not be overdone, for the less distraction to the dog's concentration, the better. If and when the dog strays off track, the handler should not allow the dog to pull him off the line of scent. By taking the strain of the lead, and with the minimum necessary tone to have the desired effect for the nature of the particular dog, quietly say 'No!' Following the gentle vocal correction, praise must be given once the dog is on the track again. If the dog lunges forward, the handler should take the strain, slowing the dog to a more reasonable pace. If the dog is disinterested it can be encouraged to put its nose down by the handler bending over and pointing to the line of the track whilst he gives the command in a pleasant manner ensuring that praise is given whenever the dog responds. At no time should the lead be jerked, nor should anything be done that is likely to break the dog's concentration. The handler must also avoid any physical or vocal act which might give the impression to the dog that he should be submissive. Tracking cannot be taught under duress. When the dog reaches the article and identifies it and picks it up, he should be given lavish praise and the handler should then remove the harness and throw the article for the dog to retrieve as a reward. This reward retrieve should be quite informal, without any kind of present or finish.

The same exercise can now be repeated on a fresh piece of land, at least fifty yards upwind of the first track, to ensure that the dog does not detect a windscent from the previous track. Each dog will vary in the number of times this exercise can be repeated in any one session without becoming bored. The handler should ensure that training ceases before possible boredom sets in. As a rough guide, four or five elementary tracks are quite sufficient for the first few lessons.

Very quickly, and possibly after the first tracking session, it is more advantageous for the handler to lay his own tracks, using the assistant to hold the dog a few yards behind the starting pole or by tying the dog to something convenient nearby. The reason being that the handler will have a more intimate knowledge of exactly where he has walked and should therefore be able to react when necessary with more certainty and speed whilst working the dog. The rate of progress depends on the dog and how quickly he gets the idea, but once he can proficiently follow the twenty-five yard track, gradual increases should be made in the degree of difficulty. The distance should be progressively increased up to a hundred yards, but still in a straight line, and by this time the handler or track-layer should have gradually reverted to normal length paces.

So far I have made no mention of what the dog should do once he has located the article. There are several schools of thought on this subject. Some prefer the dog to go down beside the article without touching it. This is one of the more common methods of track article identification used by the police, who prefer the article not to be touched or mouthed by the dog. It avoids the possible destruction of any evidence connected with it. An argument used against this method is that if the article happens to be similar to other natural articles in the vicinity, which article is the correct one? Another method is for the dog to pick up the article and stand still until the handler rejoins the dog and takes it. Alternatively, the dog can pick up and go down with the article in his mouth. For a civilian dog and handler, I do not think it matters, and I train my own dogs either to pick up and stand still and hold, or pick up, hold and go down. I choose the method which more readily adapts itself to the particular dog. The main point which the civilian Trials competitor should bear in mind is that the dog stays exactly where he has found the article so that when the handler is ready for the dog to re-commence tracking there is no question of from where the dog should start.

If the dog is well versed in the stay or stand command, then it might easily be adapted for use when finding the article. In this case the handler would need to use two commands. Immediately the dog indicates that he has found the article, he should be praised and given the 'Hold' command gently, in a non-submissive manner. As the dog responds, the 'Stand' or 'Stay' command should be given. Under no circumstances should the retrieve command of 'Fetch' be used as this will encourage the dog to return to the handler rather than remaining where he found the article. Should the handler require the dog just to drop beside the the article, then he must praise him for locating the article prior to giving the 'Down' command, with just a sufficient force of tone to encourage the dog to do so. If, on the other hand, the handler requires the dog to hold and go down, then the command 'Hold' followed by 'Down' should be given following the praise for finding the article. No matter what method is used, once that favourite last article has been found, the harness should be removed and the article thrown as a reward.

Once the dog is tracking and the length of the track is being increased, the tracks should be laid with the wind as this helps to keep the dog's nose close to the ground rather than carrying it higher to pick up windscent. In the more advanced stages of tracking, the ability of the dog to keep his nose close to the ground will become essential.

The handler can now change to a longer lead or line of about eight to ten feet, with the dog working at the extremity of the line. This should be kept taut with the dog pulling and the handler keeping constant pressure on the line. The speed should be natural to that particular dog and also comfortable for the handler who should not be forced into running behind the dog to keep up. The length of this straight track should be gradually increased to 100 yards, and as the dog progresses minor natural distractions should not worry the dog who by now should be more intent on his nosework than the passing of a bird or any natural country sound. Depending upon the nature of the dog, it can be advantageous to start using a second article on the 100 yard track, the last article remaining to be the one with which the dog is familiar. If the dog appears to start losing a little concentration on this longer track, the location of an extra article halfway along the track can act as further incentive for the dog to concentrate on the remainder of the track. Once it has found the first article, the location procedure that is used for the familiar article should be adopted without removing the harness or throwing the article. The handler must give as much praise as possible, but care should be taken not to over-excite the dog. The handler, having taken the article from the dog and quietly and calmly pocketed it, can indicate the continuation of the track whilst he encourages the dog to resume working by using the normal 'Track' command.

Now that a second article has been introduced, it is advisable whilst still at this elementary stage, that it should not be easily identifiable to the dog by sight, but at the same time not too small to become difficult. It is also preferable that this article does not contain canine scent, having never been picked up by a dog before. It must be remembered that up until now the dog has been finding a familiar article containing his own scent and that of the track-layer, and in competition it is unlikely that the article will contain anything other than its natural scent plus the scent of the track-layer.

Under no circumstances should the dog be chastised for its inability to locate the article. It is far better for the handler to ignore the fact that the dog has missed the article, letting the dog continue tracking. Chastisement can cause an unwanted association of discomfort whilst tracking, and commonsense says that if the dog missed the article it cannot be punished for something of which it is ignorant. It would be better for the handler to use a slightly larger or more suitable article next time, ensuring that the dog is adequately rewarded upon location.

Turns can now be introduced into the track pattern, and it is advisable that the handler should commence using a full-length tracking line of approximately twelve yards in length. Details of the art of line handling can be found on pages 81 to 83. It is usually best to go straight to a right-angle turn, initially laying the first leg across the wind, with the turn into the wind. This assists the dog in the transition from a straight line to a turn, and as quickly as possible the handler should change to the turn being laid with the wind, the latter being adopted immediately should the dog wind-scent the turn and cut the corner. The handler must be absolutely certain when his dog has reached the point where the turn was made, making certain that he knows every inch of the path he has trodden. Whilst it is safe to let the dog overshoot the turn by about a yard, providing he works out the turn by himself, the handler should not let the dog overshoot too far, ensuring that he does not by gently applying pressure on the line at the appropriate moment. If the dog negotiates the turn without the necessity of casting, then so much the better. If, however, the dog casts, he should be allowed to do so without undue pressure being applied to the line, but it is preferable that the line should remain taut. As soon as he locates the track again, praise should be given. The handler must now drill himself always to stand still on the spot once the dog loses the track and starts casting round to find it again. Whilst the handler knows exactly where the turn or turns are, there is of course no need for him to move until he receives a definite correct indication of the change of direction from the dog.

At any stage of tracking, particularly when the track has been laid by someone else and without prior knowledge of its shape by the handler, he must stand still and resist any temptation to wander from that point until the dog takes the turn. The only exception to this rule is if the handler is convinced that the dog has overshot the turn by more than the length of the tracking line. In this case the handler should retrace his steps to the point of the turn and cast the dog again. Many good dogs are ruined by inexperienced handlers following the dog rather than standing still when it starts hunting for the turn, and hunting with its nose up is usually resorted to by the inexperienced dog. With practice, the dog learns to keep its nose to the ground to pick up the track.

At first, a hundred-yard first leg, and a fifty-yard second leg, is quite sufficient with one article being laid halfway along the first leg, and another article being laid at the end of the second leg. Assuming that the dog is acting spontaneously in the required manner when finding its usual familiar article, strange articles can now be used at the end of the track. The last article should however be large enough to ensure that the dog finds it, so that the normal praise and the throwing routine can continue. Thus, to the dog, the track is happily concluded.

Once the dog is consistently successful in negotiating the one turn, a second right-angle turn can be introduced, making the track pattern three sides of a square, each leg being approximately a hundred yards long. The handler should vary this at each session by laying left and right turns, with the wind coming from different directions. Once the dog has mastered the three-sided track, tracks can be run progressively older, starting with a five-minute time lag between laying and running, with an extra five minutes being added as the dog consistently completes the younger track with success. Gradual increases in the angle of some of the turns can also be incorporated until the dog is capable of negotiating a very acute turn. A balance between the increase of angle and increase of time lag should be maintained, it being unwise to add fifteen minutes to the time lag plus a much more acute angle than the relatively inexperienced dog has been accustomed to so far.

By now considerable progress has been made and the handler should be developing the most important aspect of tracking, the knowledge that makes the dog and handler a team, and that is the art of reading the dog. Right from the first tracking lesson the handler should have studiously watched the dog whilst it is working, learning every little indication it gives under certain circumstances. For instance, the way the dog carries its head, a movement of the shoulders, the action of the tail or ears. Each dog has its own characteristics, which, when studied, will tell the handler when the dog is at a turn, or an article, or at a cross track, etc. There are no hard and fast rules, just painstaking study of one's own dog. In competition the handler has no knowledge of the direction of the track or the location of the articles and can only rely on the messages the dog transmits in the form of body movements and characteristics. I cannot over-stress this point as being one of the most important lessons a handler must learn. It only comes with experience which is gained whilst studiously watching the dog's reactions on tracks the handler knows, having laid them himself.

The dog should now be at a stage where gradual increases are being made in time lag, number of turns, and degree of difficulty of turns. It should be stressed again that the handler must not rush the dog by making the track more difficult than it is capable of completing successfully. As in all dog training, go back a stage if the dog is struggling on a more difficult track than that which it has previously been set. The angles can gradually become more acute and the legs more numerous, but from experience I find it better not to overdo the number of turns on a practice track. If the handler consistently lays track patterns with many short legs, it is apt to make the dog get into the habit of premature casting on a straight leg. Each time the dog reaches a tricky patch, where for some reason the scent is not holding too well, because he has been brainwashed into expecting frequent turns he will cast for a possible turn rather than work on a little further, finding that in fact the track continues in a straight line. It is far better to lay a long straight line every now and again, just as it is occasionally to go back to running younger tracks.

Assuming the dog has mastered his obedience and agility exercises and is now capable of handling a thirty-minute-old track of about ten legs including acute turns, the handler will almost be ready to enter the dog in its first Utility Dog Stake, but not quite. The unknown and unpredictable is always to be found at a trial, so the dog needs to have encountered and mastered cross-tracks. When training against crosstracks (see Figure 2), the handler should always watch both the correct track and the cross-track being laid so that he is completely aware of just where the interference occurs. He can, of course, lay the correct track himself. Once the dog has been successfully trained to complete half-hour-old tracks, the first few crosstrack training lessons should have a crosstrack half an hour older or younger than the correct track. The reason being that part of the identity of any track is the amount of scent that it holds by reasons of age. A crosstrack laid at almost the same time as the correct track is in theory more difficult for the dog than that which is older or younger. When the dog works the track the handler should observe closely the reactions of the dog as it approaches the interference. Whilst it is very nice for the dog to ignore the crosstrack completely, as a

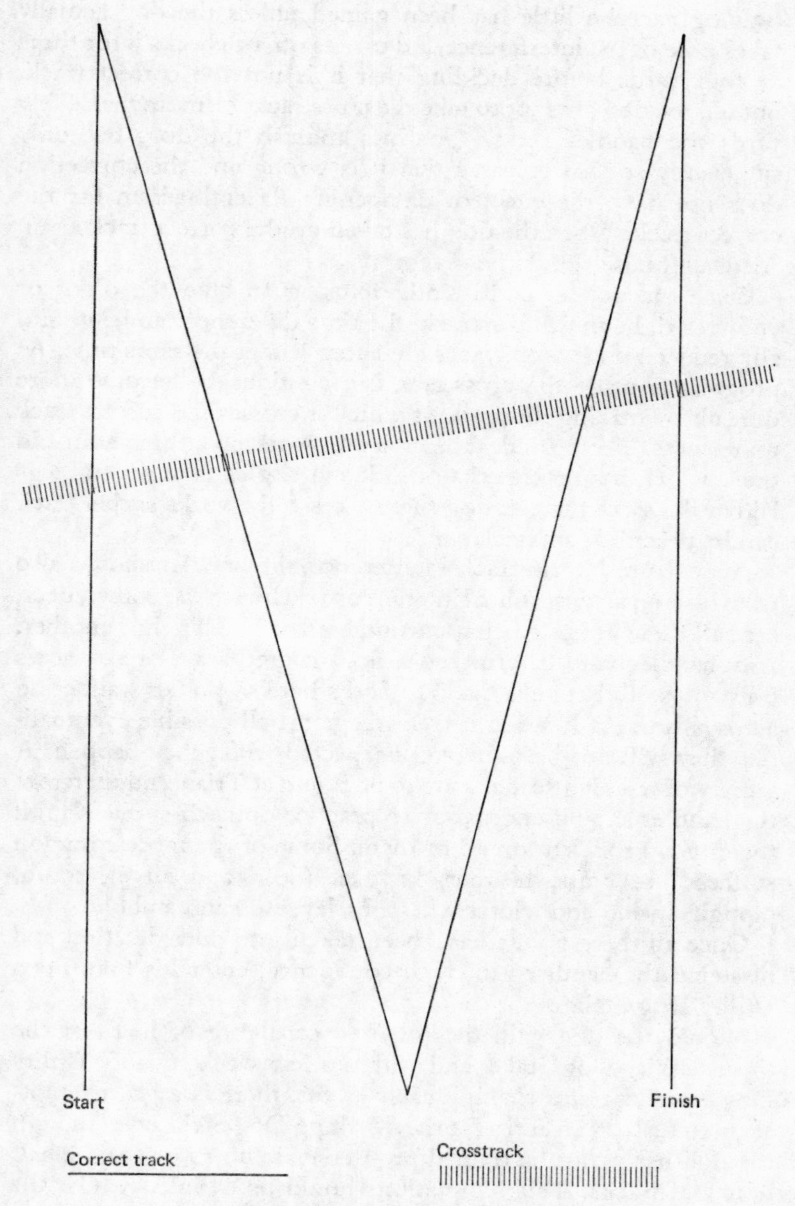

Fig. 2 Training against crosstracks

training exercise little has been gained unless the dog actually takes note of the interference and carries on, or checks it for three or four yards before deciding that it is not the correct track. Should the dog attempt to take the crosstrack for more than a few yards the handler should gently admonish the dog, but only sufficiently so that it learns that it is wrong and the correction does not have the effect of dampening its enthusiasm for the correct track. When the dog has taken up the correct track again adequate praise should be given.

Once the dog is consistently refusing to take the older or younger right-angle crosstrack, the time difference can be gradually reduced until both tracks are being laid at the same time. As progress is made the crosstrack can continue to become more difficult by making the angle at which it crosses the correct track more acute. The final ideal being a dog working a three-hour-old track which has crosstracks of different angles over several legs laid at the same time. A dog that successfully works such a track can be described as 'track sure'.

Apart from human track interference, the handler should also train his dog against animal interference such as cows, ponies, deer, etc., all these animals being encountered at one Trial or another. Any handler who has tracked a dog in the New Forest knows only too well that he is likely to find a herd of ponies wandering across his track. If a dog is trained against all possible eventualities they will not be quite so unexpected when they happen. A variety of tracking surfaces are to be found at Trials and therefore the handler should endeavour to practice on such surfaces until the dog is proficient on all of them. Some of the more common surfaces are grass, heather, bracken (dead and alive), scrub, plough, spring and winter wheat, barley, etc., and stubble.

Once all these points have been taken into consideration and mastered the handler can, with confidence, enter his first Open Utility Dog Stake.

Should the dog gain the required certificate of merit at the Open Utility Dog Stake, and within a few weeks qualify Utility Dog Excellent at a championship event, there is a great temptation to rush off an entry for the Working Dog Stake even though the dog has yet to be trained progressively up to one-and-a-half hour-old tracks. This temptation should be avoided whilst the handler gradually increases the time lag and the dog can master tracks in excess of one-and-a-half hours old. The same applies to the transition from the Working Dog Stake to the Tracking Dog Stake where the time lag is three hours. A golden rule of all dog training is that successful completion of an easier stage of an exercise is a step forward as opposed to partial completion of a more difficult stage which is a retrograde step. The handler should, therefore, revert to the previous degree of difficulty any time the dog is found to be struggling. It also helps to maintain a dog's tracking confidence if it is given a younger and therefore easier track soon after failure of something more difficult.

During a dog's early tracking career and before entry into the Utility Dog Stake, minor distractions should be encountered by the dog, such as a track-layer laying a track in an adjacent field, gunfire from another stake, which could be as close as one hundred yards. Two people, to simulate the track-layer and the judge, can be used to follow the dog and handler at a discreet distance with a leg turning back towards them, thus making them quite visible to the dog. A car starting up outside the field being worked by the dog is another possible hazard to an easily distractable dog. The handler can probably think of other distractions, but care should always be maintained to ensure that the distraction is not of a sufficient degree to cause an association of fear whilst the dog is tracking. However, the keen tracker dog will take all of these distractions in his stride, ignoring them completely.

To avoid the dog having a preconceived idea of the track by using its memory, tracks should always be laid on a variety of sites. Articles should never be laid on a turn or there is a risk that the dog will associate an article with a turn. Neither should they consistently be left by trees or prominent markers. It is also bad practice to lay tracks continually with legs near to the extremity of the land, such as a few feet away from a hedge. Whilst these things are useful as markers for the handler when laying the tracks, they are likely to build up in the dog an unwanted association of ideas, such as continually following hedges and looking for articles beside natural markers. If the handler wishes to use a tree as a marker for an article, it is better that he carries on walking a certain number of paces after the tree before dropping the article.

To train a dog up to and beyond the standard of tracking

required in the Tracking Dog Stake is only a case of gradual increases in the degree of difficulty, such as longer time lags, smaller articles, more frequent and more acute turns. Providing that the handler has trained the dog correctly in the basics of tracking and that both the handler and the dog are suitable material, a good tracking dog is purely a matter of time and patience. It should be remembered that Tracking Dog Stake judges are likely to use all kinds of articles, some being as small as $\frac{1}{16}$ inch plastic coated wire no more than two or three inches long, and articles that are natural to the ground. Stones, twigs, bark, fircones, conkers, etc., have all been used in the past and are likely to be used in the future. Such articles should occasionally be used in training the experienced dog, but there is no harm in using a larger article for the majority of practice tracks. The tracker dog should also be given younger tracks to work rather than continually working three-hour-old tracks.

At a Working Trial there are always a high percentage of dogs that complete the track but have not found sufficient articles to qualify. In the Utility Dog Stake the recovery of an article is not a pre-requisite for qualification and this very fact can lull the beginner handler into a false sense of security. At all times maximum importance should be placed upon the location and recovery of articles by the dog. Failure by the handler to ensure that this golden rule is observed during the dog's early tracking career can lead to disappointment in the more advanced stakes.

In the Utility Dog Stake one article is left at the end of the track. In the Working Dog and Police Dog Stakes two articles are left on the track, one of which must be recovered to ensure qualification, whilst in the Tracking Dog Stake three articles are left on the track and a minimum of two of these articles must be recovered. In the UD Stake up to fifteen marks are allotted to the article, and in all other stakes up to ten marks are awarded for recovery of each article. It can immediately be seen that great importance is placed upon recovery of articles, and rightly so. Ask any competitor in championship TD if he thinks he is going to win the Working Trial Certificate when after every dog has completed the nosework there are those dogs who have recovered more track or search articles than his own dog. Maybe he knows that he has an outside chance of the other dogs' failing completely on the remaining parts of the stake still to be judged, but he also knows that being ten or more marks behind other dogs virtually rules out his dog from being the winner of that Trial.

I have been asked by handlers with dogs in the WD or TD Stakes how to improve their dogs on indicating and recovering articles. I am usually tempted to pass on a witty and somewhat sarcastic comment once made by a very great and respected dog trainer who, when asked a similar question about a fault developed in basic training answered, 'I don't know how to correct the fault for I never let it occur in the first place.' Behind that reply lies a sound piece of wisdom. Think about it. Being somewhat cautious on the subject of dog training I have so far resisted the temptation to make such a remark, for inevitably that same handler would see me complete a track with my dog having insufficient articles to qualify.

With dogs who are poor on article indication the first thing to do, as with all dog training faults, is establish why the fault has occured. Usually it will be found that the handler has placed too much emphasis on the track, to the detriment of article indication, thus making the dog what is known as 'track happy'. A track happy dog is only interested in tracking, and articles are of no consequence to him. When this fault is already apparent the handler should be using four or five articles on each track which are of sufficient size to ensure that the dog finds them en route, but not too large for him to find by sight alone. If this ploy alone does not cure the problem and the handler has a keen retrieving dog, then as each of these largish articles are recovered the handler can quickly join his dog and give it a quick retrieve of say one yard's distance. With the dog I handle in Trials at present I use a large rubber ring which is his favourite toy for tug-of-war games. Any time that I think he is getting slack on track article indication I make the rubber ring the first article of the practice track and when he finds it we have a quick ten seconds' tug-of-war game, then I pocket the ring and tell him to continue tracking. Immediately the dog shows a marked enthusiasm to find the next article. Again, by doing so, or by giving the dog a quick short sharp retrieve, we have turned training into a game, and that makes for happier working dogs anyway. However, a word of caution, the handler can easily overdo such methods to the extent where the dog will only wish to keep playing with that article rather than tracking on when the handler requires him to do so. You, the handler, must be the judge of how far you can take such games. Another ploy is to use food as bait, placing the food next to or underneath the article, but again great care must be exercised or the greedy type of dog will finish up as one who will only work for food.

Whilst many hints on training can be given in a book, the real art of dog training is knowing when to take, or not to take, certain action and how far one can go without causing additional problems. Such knowledge distinguishes the great dog handlers from the mediocre and cannot be taught. It is instinctive.

Part of a dog's tracking training should include training against back-tracking (see Figure 3). Many a dog has gone wrong at the beginning of a track, picked up the end of the track and then back-tracked to the starting pole. Careful training can teach a dog to distinguish between tracking forward and back-tracking. When a dog is proficient at a thirty-minute-old track, lay some practice tracks that have no start pole and approach the first leg from such a position that it will give the dog the chance to go either way along the first leg. If the dog does back-track his tracking will usually be much less positive than when tracking forward, and the handler should quickly learn to read the difference in the dog's tracking attitude. This will enable the handler to suspect that the dog is back-tracking in competition. When the dog attempts to take the back-track in practice, gently admonish him for doing so and encourage him to track forward. This admonishment should be just sufficient to correct that particular dog and not so as to ensure unwanted apprehension. Again the art of dog training, the handler must decide what is too much or too little correction for that particular dog. After several lessons in training against back-tracking the dog will learn the difference and will be unlikely to take you round the track backwards.

All these aids to better tracking are carried out with the handler laying his own tracks, and I cannot over-stress my conviction that the handler should lay nine out of ten of his own tracks. Every time the handler has a practice track laid without any knowledge of exactly where the track is, that handler takes a risk of the dog failing, and failure in any exercise in dog training is an unwanted retrograde step. On the other hand, every time the dog succeeds in practice some progress must have been made. So

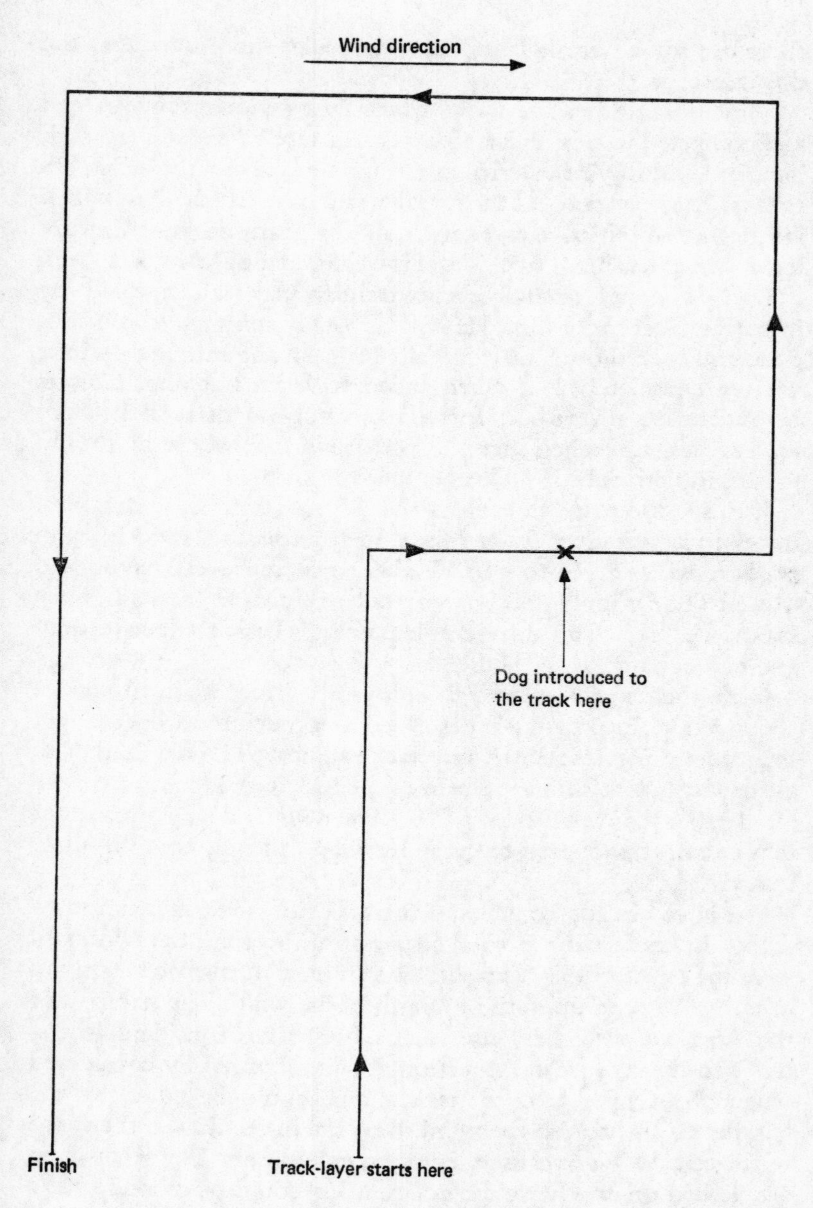

Fig. 3 Training against back-tracking

therefore my advice is lay your own tracks and ensure that the dog succeeds.

Sometimes a dog and handler who have previously only trained and competed in Obedience Competitions will decide to try their hand at Working Trials. Providing that this previous training has been skilfully carried out the handler will have left the dog with a fair degree of initiative and should not have any additional problems when teaching tracking. However, a dog that has been bored by unenlightened obedience training may well have had any initiative taken from him. He will be totally submissive and subdued and even though he originally had a strong retrieve instinct, will be completely lost when asked to learn tracking. This is because he has always been forced to act only on instructions from his handler, and when asked to perform a task where he should use his initiative, he is no longer able to do so.

If this is the case the handler should not attempt any tracking but use play retrieves for training. Such retrieves should bear no relation whatsoever to formal obedience retrieves, having no wait at the beginning and no present or finish at the end. They should be just a game to re-kindle the dog's basic retrieve instinct and enthusiasm for the chase.

Once the dog has started to enjoy this game, again he can be set on a track as previously described, but much more encouragement to put his nose down and track might well be required. The elementary track should remain elementary until the dog can be encouraged to work forward on his own and any premature temptation to move on to greater things will only result in utter disaster.

We have already considered the effect of wind in relation to scent dispersal. Prior to total dispersal of the scent the wind will have the effect of displacing it. The amount of displacement will of course depend upon the strength of the wind. The strength of the wind can also carry the scent of articles a considerable distance so therefore wind direction should be carefully considered when planning a practice track. Care should be taken by the handler to ensure that the wind direction in relation to the shape of the track will not cause the dog to cut corners. The scent of an article laid on another close adjacent leg could be carried to the dog if the wind was very strong. Figure 4 shows the right and wrong way to lay a track in such conditions.

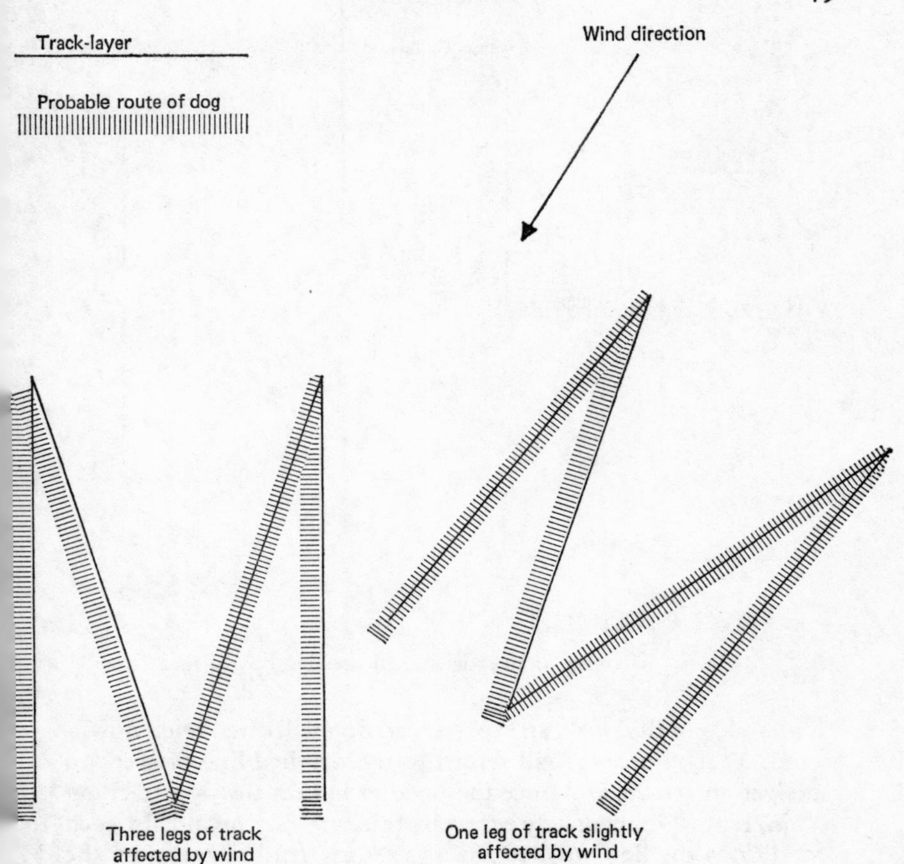

Fig.4 Some effects of wind on tracks

An experienced Working Trials handler should be able to lay a track in a field and three hours later return to that field and retrace the track perfectly, knowing exactly when he is about to come across an article. In other words, a perfect knowledge of that track is required not only if it is being laid for someone else in competition, but also if it is a practice track for that handler's own dog. With such detailed knowledge of the track a handler has every chance of doing and saying the right things at the right time, and a good tracking dog could be the result. However the handler must not be fooled by the dog that tracks wide of the original line taken by the track-layer. When the wind is blowing

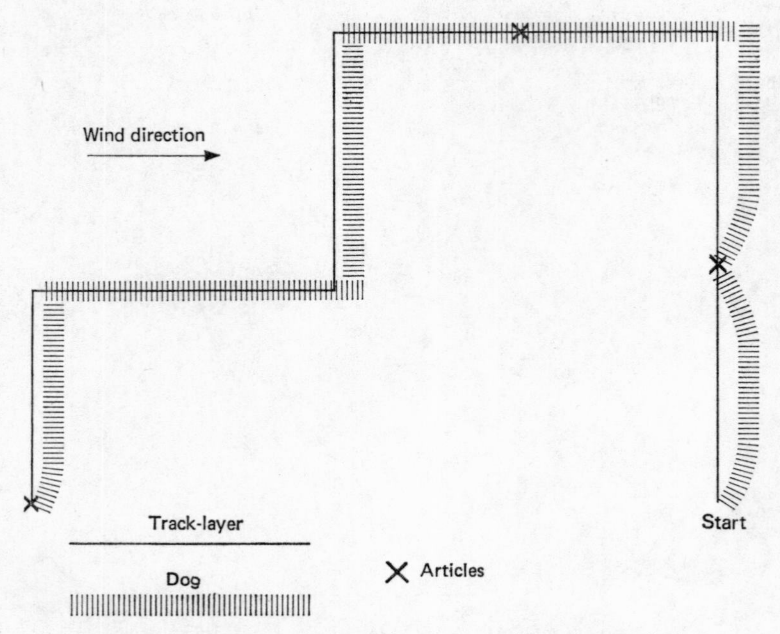

Fig. 5 Recovery of an article when tracking down wind

across a leg of the track, an experienced dog will often track downwind. That same dog will return to the original line of scent to recover an article, and once the handler has set the dog tracking again, he will immediately revert to tracking downwind. In such conditions the dog will remain on the original line taken by the track-layer when the dog takes a turn which is into the wind, or with the wind. As the dog takes further turns on to legs that have the wind blowing across them the dog will again revert to tracking downwind. Figure 5 demonstrates the line a dog might take in such conditions. A dog tracking downwind can be as much as three feet away from the original line taken by the track-layer, but the distance will depend upon the strength of the wind and the time lapse since the track was laid.

Tracking is a fascinating and rewarding hobby, but one that requires a certain amount of dedication by the handler. It cannot be taught at home in the back garden and needs to be practised in all kinds of weather, including the weather when one feels more comfortable sitting by the fireside.

LINE HANDLING

Good line handling only comes with experience. I have already stated that a tracking line will be more of a liability than an asset to the raw beginner, but when the time comes to use a full length line the handler should have some knowledge of its use. Prior to setting the dog on the track the handler should lay the line out on the ground ensuring that it is not tangled. The harness is then put on the dog and the line attached to the 'D' ring on the rear top of the harness. Twelve yards of line is about the right length, and approximately three-quarters of it should be gathered into loops in one of the hands, the other hand being used to hold the line.

If the dog is set to work a few yards before the start pole, with any luck he will pick up the line of scent created by the track-layer where he walked to his chosen position to plant the start pole. Should the track continue in the same direction after the pole, the dog already has the advantage of being on track prior to its commencement. Even though the line of scent may go in a different direction from the pole the dog knows the track he is on prior to reaching the pole. As the dog tracks towards the pole and the line becomes taut it can be allowed to slip through the fingers of the hand that controls it until the dog is on approximately six yards of line. As the dog reaches the pole he should take the scent of the pole, or the area of scent immediately surrounding the pole, before setting off again. If the dog goes straight past the pole without stopping, providing that the handler is satisfied with the dog's tracking indication, he should not break his concentration by making him check the scent at the pole. If the dog needs to cast at the pole the handler should be standing one or two yards behind the pole allowing the dog to cast on six or seven yards of line. The line can be tight but should not be below the level of the dog's back. The tension of the line is controlled by the handler re-looping the line in the carrying hand if the dog lessens the distance between the handler whilst casting, and by paying out the line through the fingers when more is required again. As the dog picks up the track the handler should set off behind the dog who is now on about eight yards of line. There is a school of thought that prefers the line to be laid out on the ground behind the handler as the dog commences to track, but I feel this is a dangerous practice for two reasons. It is all very well and good on grassland, but if the tracking land contains a lot of scrub and small bushes, it can become snagged, thus causing a sudden jerking of the line which may badly distract the more sensitive dog. The other reason is the possibility of the dog's feet becoming entangled in the line whilst casting behind the handler at the start pole.

At all times the line should be kept reasonably tight and not allowed to trail upon the ground. The degree of tension will depend upon the nature of the dog. Some keen dogs pull heavily on the line thus making it extremely taut, other dogs work on a slightly slack line. The same reasons apply for keeping the line between dog and handler from trailing on the ground whilst tracking as they do for the commencement of the track, also the possibility that a trailing line may be interfering with the scent of the track, particularly when the dog is casting. If the handler has the dog tracking normally on seven or eight yards of line, at any time the dog casts, the handler has a few yards of line in reserve should the dog start to take a different angle without giving the usual clear indication of a turn. When this happens the handler can pay out more line and remain standing exactly where he is, and by the time the line has gone to the full extent, he should be certain by the indications the dog is giving whether or not he should follow him. If the handler decides that the dog is not yet correct he can gently ease the casting dog back towards him, thus regaining a few spare yards of line again. On the other hand, if the handler is satisfied and sets off behind the dog, he should walk slightly faster than the speed of the dog for a few yards and regain the spare few yards of line. It should be easily seen that if the handler had the full length of line out, when the dog casts and then moves off again, having no line in reserve the handler has no option but to move from the spot at which he was last certain that the dog was correct. After a few yards the dog may decide that it is wrong and commence casting again, and the handler has now moved from the correct place at which to cast. In this situation not only is the handler likely to get lost, but he may be putting his own tracks across the correct line of the turn, thus causing more confusion for the dog. Every time that a handler follows his dog when it is wrong he is increasing the chance of it becoming less tracksure. If the handler has learned to read his dog and has line in reserve, then the chances of this happening are minimized.

The foregoing is based on using land that does not have undue amounts of undergrowth, bushes, trees, etc. When the handler is faced with such land he should work with a shorter line to suit the conditions, even to the point where he is holding the line directly above his head with the dog a yard ahead of him, but this extremity would only be so in dense, waist or chest high, undergrowth.

Perfection of line handling is an art, and after many years' practice, a good handler will find that at all times he has the line under control and is as adept with its use as a cowboy is with a lassoo. It cannot be over-stressed that good line handling is an asset to the dog and poor line handling a liability. We therefore revert to the old argument that for every good dog there are ninety-nine bad handlers.

THE SEARCH

The ideal factors that go towards making a good search team of man and dog are the ability of the dog to work enthusiastically and to retrieve cleanly and accurately; the ability of the handler to read the dog, direct him with the minimum of fuss, and work the dog in the search area so that he has every chance of success. Like many things, a perfectly worked search by man and dog looks very simple – it is only those that are less than perfection that look difficult. With rare exceptions, the searches that look simple have been worked by a team that has started with the right basic training and continued correctly from thereon.

To get a keen searcher is relatively simple if we start with a dog having a strong retrieve instinct and make few mistakes. Before serious search training is commenced it is advisable that the dog is capable of executing a formal controlled retrieve. Although the search is not required to be carried out in this manner, the degree of control required to achieve a formal retrieve will stand the handler in good stead. For example, it was necessary to teach the dog to 'hold' on command at a distance, and such control will be necessary with the search whilst possible confusion in the dog's mind is minimized. The handler who erroneously attempts to train a dog to search without having taught basic retrieve control is taking great risks of confusing the dog. For example, what can that handler do to encourage and help the dog once he has found the article? Commands that are not yet understood will not only be useless but will serve to introduce confusion. It will do no harm once again to remind the reader that confusion often leads to apprehension.

Assuming that your dog has been taught to retrieve, even though he may do so naturally, and that you have some method of commanding the dog to pick up and hold, i.e. the 'Hold' command, then search training can commence. Like most training it is best taught as a game which the handler can play with the dog whilst exercising him. The dog's favourite toy is the obvious choice as his first article, and this can be thrown into the long grass beside the hedgerows, etc. First play with the dog and article, and then he should be allowed to see you throw the article so that the thrill of the chase will induce enthusiasm. Once the article has landed, preferably so that it will only become visible when the dog is within one or two feet of it, let him go and give him the chosen search command such as 'Find' or 'Search'. Encourage him as he finds it, and if necessary use the 'Hold' command to get him to pick up the article and the 'Retrieve' command to get him to return to you. The reader will no doubt remember that for a formal retrieve at this stage we would give the 'present' signal to the dog, which is drawing the hands towards the groin. By leaving out this signal the handler can safely use the retrieve command for the dog to return with the article and take it from him whilst he is still standing. No confusion will arise in the dog's mind as to whether he should or should not present if this signal is left out. Whilst the dog is returning with the article the handler should watch him closely, and at the first sign of the article being dropped, the handler should use the 'Hold' command to remind the dog not to do so. This play search into the long grass, etc. can be done several times, but should be suspended before boredom sets in.

From this stage of training the logical progression is to replace the dog's toy with articles of a size suitable to the ground, i.e. not too large as to be seen by the dog, and not too small to be an article even an experienced dog would have difficulty in locating. When the dog is consistently mastering these games the handler can set up four poles to create a search area. The ground should be foiled to create an area of scent and to avoid any possibility of a track to the article. Initially it would be advisable for the handler to revert to the dog's favourite toy, throwing it into the area, and once the dog has seen it land, letting him find and retrieve as was done previously. If this is successful, for the next step the dog should not be allowed to see the article thrown. Further progression is to revert to other articles again, but continue to throw them into the area. To act as a transition from thrown articles to those which are going to be placed in the area unseen by the dog, it is best to place several articles in the area and then throw one into the area in sight of the dog. Once he has retrieved the thrown article the handler can pretend to throw the article again and encourage the dog to go and look for it. Once the dog will do this we can gradually progress to a search as carried out in competition, and by such methods as described a controlled search will be the result.

To speed up an already bored lethargic dog is much more difficult than to get it right the first time. Like most of dog training, little, often and right, is one of the secrets. The lethargic dog has probably already associated four search poles with utter boredom and therefore the handler should do away with the formality of a laid-out search area, instead training should be turned into a game that is played in very short bursts. Lots of fun, plenty of encouragement and lavish praise, with the article being thrown in sight of the dog into the edges of hedgerows or ground with sufficient cover to conceal it. In other words, back to the beginning – a golden rule of dog training, and so often overlooked by the handler.

Another mistake made is for the handler to stand outside the search area supposedly bored to tears with the whole thing. This type of handler will often wonder why the dog seems bored as well. It is no strange coincidence that the smart handler often has a smart dog.

When searching, much more attention to detail could be used by many handlers. So many just test the wind direction purely as a formality which they hope will please the judge, when, with thought, the handler can give the dog quite a lot of assistance. Having tested the wind direction, the handler should then survey the area and make certain decisions. By looking at Figure 6 it can be seen that the wind will be blowing the scent of the judge, steward, spectators, etc. into and across the search area. Whilst it

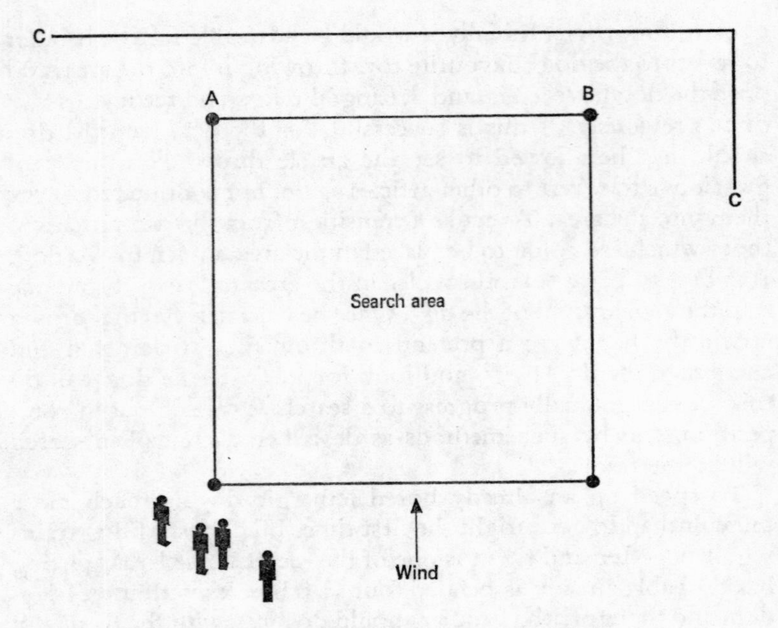

Fig. 6 Searching in relation to the wind

is quite impossible for the dog to search the area under such conditions, in competition it would be preferable to ask these people if they would move. In Figure 6 anywhere along the line 'C' would be a safe place to ask them to stand, and by doing so the possibility of additional unwanted scent in the area has been removed and is therefore one less distraction for the dog. By studying this diagram the reader can see that the dog would have the best chance if he was sent directly into the wind from outside line 'A' to 'B' or across the area from outside of point 'B'. I stress *outside* for many handlers stand on the line which has two main disadvantages. If the judge has laid an article on the line marked 'A B' and the handler stands on the edge of the area, the wind direction is such to virtually ensure that the dog will not receive a windborne scent of the article. Should the dog locate and retrieve an article from the area and is prone to dropping articles at the handler's feet, with the handler standing on the edge, the article is going to fall back into the search area. If the handler is standing four or five feet back from the edge of the area, both of these problems are overcome. The dog has a chance to find the downwind article and the article dropped by the dog just prior to reaching the handler is now outside the search area. Therefore valuable time is not lost by directing the dog to search for the article again, the handler can pick it up instead.

Needless to say, a dropped article is not the perfect way for the dog to retrieve from the search area, but if the dog is going to drop it, it must be preferable for the article to drop outside the area. It may well be that the ground is rough and therefore the article is lost. In such a case I would advise the handler to mark the place where the article fell with his hat or anything handy, for time is precious in the search exercise. The dog can then continue working the area and the handler can recover the lost article after time has been called.

Throughout this book I have tried to stress the importance of perfecting basic exercises, and I make no apology for stressing once again that dropping or mouthing articles is not a search fault, it is a retrieve fault. Do not chastise the dog if he drops articles whilst training. It is far better for the handler to try and correct the fault by going back to retrieve training with search type articles. Another common mistake is for the handler to be so thrilled when the dog recovers the articles and so concerned about the time factor that the process of delivery of the article to the handler and the subsequent praise and return to the area is very much rushed. A few extra seconds are wisely spent quietly and calmly taking the article from the dog with vocal and physical praise, this should be done efficiently but unhurriedly. The handler should then send the dog back to continue searching without any sign of panic being transmitted to the dog.

The handler can assist the dog by moving quietly around the search area ensuring that the dog covers every part by directing him when necessary. However there is a great art in directing the dog economically and only when necessary. The same applies to encouragement, for it is possible to do both things at the wrong time which may have the effect of distracting the dog just as he was likely to indicate an article.

Remember that in all stakes, marks are allotted for style and control. Judges differ with their interpretation, but I prefer to split the marks – one half for the style of the dog, and the other half for the control of the dog by the handler. For full marks for style,

I would expect the dog to work throughout the five minutes in a quiet steady manner, retrieving and delivering to hand quite cleanly after locating articles. For control, I would want to see the dog respond correctly to every command by the handler, but at the same time that handler should only intrude into the dog's concentration when necessary.

The directional control in the search area is a very important part of the exercise, to which insufficient attention is paid by many Trials handlers. I am a great believer in minimizing the possibility of any confusion entering the dog's mind. From that premise I prefer to have, as near as is possible, perfect directional control with the dog prior to search training commencing. If, by one command and/or signal, the handler can convey his requirements immediately to the dog, this must be preferable to the handler who needs several commands before the dog understands. Again we are trying to eliminate confusion. Not only do we need to be able to turn the dog left or right and to be able to send it on, but also to be able to turn the dog around on command. For instance, if the dog is working away from the handler and going towards the far side of the area, as the dog leaves the area a simple command which will turn the dog around whilst he continues working is advantageous. It is dangerous practice to use his recall command for this purpose, for having done so and turned the dog back into the square, the handler will expect the dog to continue working and the dog will expect to return to the handler, once again a risk of confusion to the dog. I found with one of my dogs that two quick claps of the hand would turn him back into the area and this is what I use, as it had the desired effect and I do not believe in teaching the dog something for teaching's sake.

The size of the articles used in training is of importance. At a Trial the Kennel Club specify that the size of the articles should be in relation to the ground, and as a guide should be no longer than a six-inch nail and no smaller than a matchbox. The reason for this wording is to allow the judge to use his own discretion according to the type of ground on which he is to judge the searches. This can vary from something approaching a bowling green for its lack of cover, to heather three feet deep. Wise is the judge who makes inquiry about the land before selecting the articles. Whilst training the dog, a handler should also give careful consideration to the articles to be used and this will depend to a large extent on the type of dog and the stage of training that has been reached. In my opinion it is quite wrong to choose articles that are so difficult that it takes the dog five minutes or more to find just one. Whilst it would not be advantageous always to provide over-large articles, a happy balance can be struck so that the dog gets used to having to work for success, with success being possible.

The positioning of the articles is also important whilst training, and just as in competition, due regard must be paid to wind direction. Any tuft or mound that will prevent the scent of the article being windborne should be avoided during early training stages.

In the section on tracking we have dealt with the importance of teamwork between dog and handler. On the handler's side much of that teamwork comes from being able to read the dog accurately. Careful study of the dog will enable the handler to understand certain characteristics displayed whilst searching the area. These characteristics will in time convey to the handler various pieces of information, such as 'I cannot find anything over here', 'I am only pretending to work, hoping that if I run around you will be quite happy', 'I am thoroughly bored and will only work harder if you insist', 'I think I can detect the scent of an article over there', 'I have found an article but do not want to pick it up', 'You think I am moving on to an article but really it is a smell that just interests me'. There are, of course, many other things that the dog can tell the handler, and painstaking study of the dog's attitude and characteristics under given circumstances will enable the dog to be read just like a book.

If you can train your dog to a standard of being able to locate and retrieve all four articles at three Trials out of four, then you can safely say that you have an excellent searching dog. Add to that a good tracking dog and you are three-quarters of the way to making him a Working Trial Champion.

5
Equipment

The Working Trial enthusiast needs to acquire a certain amount of equipment. Obviously a lead and collar are required, but it is quite amazing how little thought dog owners give to such equipment. Time and time again whilst I have been instructing at training classes, new handlers have arrived with a boisterous large breed which is being restrained by a thin piece of material, masquerading as leather, with what amounts to a bent piece of wire at the end for attaching to the dog's collar. Usually the first corrective jerk of this inferior equipment means the parting of the leather or the attaching hook. The dog may well have cost a lot of money to purchase and one can visualize him lunging forward in a crowded street, the lead parting and the dog finishing up under a bus.

The correct lead to purchase is one preferably made of good quality bridle leather or nylon webbing. It should be approximately four feet long with a handle, and have a strong trigger hook (included in Figure 7), attached to the end. The width of the lead will depend on the size of the breed of dog it is to be used to secure. An Alsatian will need at least a $\frac{7}{8}$ inch width lead, whilst the medium sized breeds should not have less than half an inch of width.

The owner may prefer the dog to wear an ordinary leather collar when not being trained. To this should be attached a disc with details of where the owner can be contacted should the dog be lost. However, for training, a check chain constructed of rustless welded links should be used. When pulled tight there should not be more than three to four inches of spare chain. During training, the dog will still be growing, so it will be necessary to purchase additional check chains as the dog outgrows the previous one.

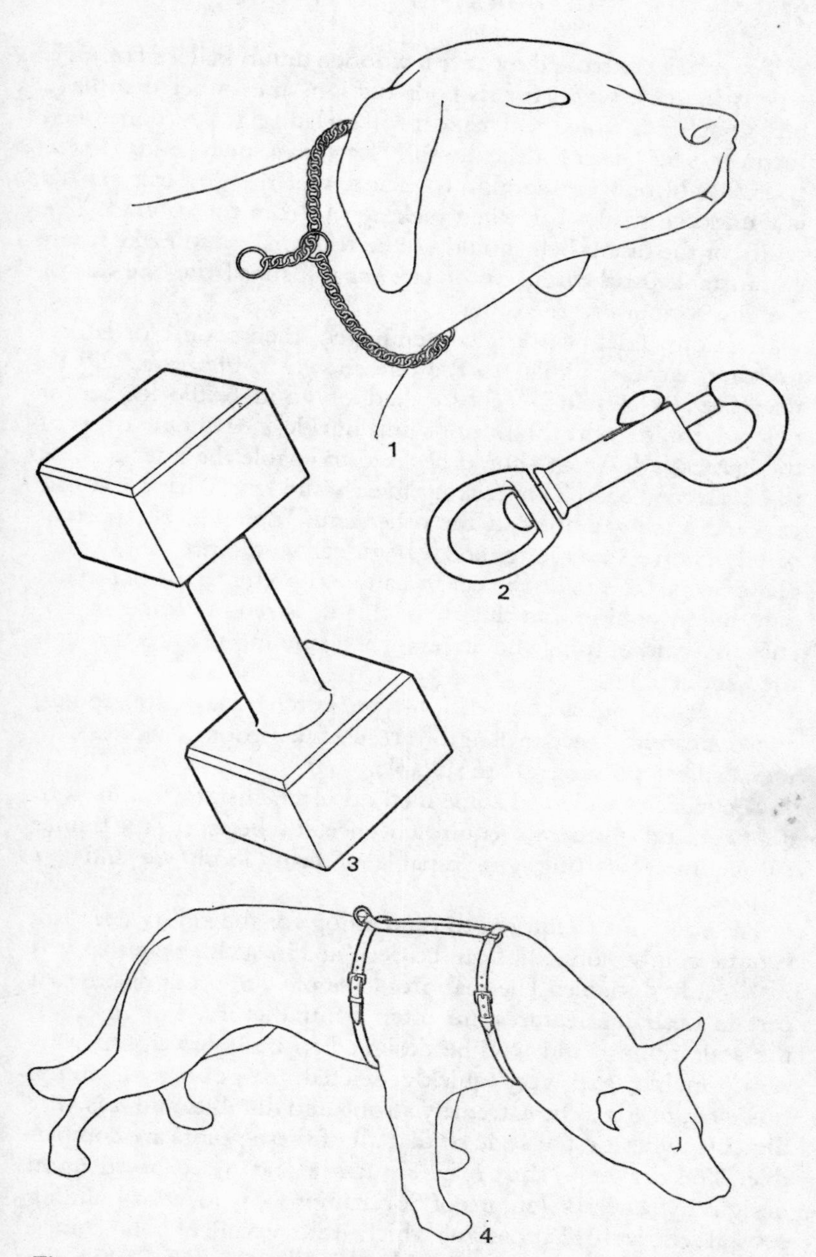

Fig. 7 Equipment: 1 check chain, 2 trigger hook, 3 dumb-bell, 4 harness

To teach a controlled retrieve a wooden dumb-bell is necessary. Ash is the best wood for its construction, and rather than have hexagonal ends which will make it roll on landing, for a controlled throw it is far better for the dumb-bell to have square ends. These ends should be large enough to ensure that the dog can get his jaw underneath the bar when picking up from the ground. The width of the dumb-bell should not be too small as to make it uncomfortable for the dog, or too large that it slips from one side of the dog's mouth to the other.

If serious Trials work is contemplated, then sooner or later a tracking harness, similar to the one shown in Figure 7, will be necessary. It should be constructed of good bridle leather or nylon webbing with brass rings and buckles. At the rear top of the harness a 'D' ring should be fixed to enable the tracking line to be fastened to it. The tracking line should have a handle at one end and a trigger hook at the other end. It should be approximately twelve yards long, and a beginner would probably find a plaited rope clothes line easier to handle. I prefer to use flat nylon parachute webbing, but the use of this does require some experience to avoid burning the fingers when running the line through the hand.

For setting out a competition-type search square, four poles, approximately 4 feet in length, are useful. Broom handles with metal spikes on the end are suitable.

The handler will need some method of practising steadiness to gunshot, and as firearms require a licence, it is better for the trainer to acquire a starting gun capable of firing both ·22 and ·32 blanks.

The equipment required to train a dog for the agility exercises is quite cumbersome, but can be designed in such a way that it is reasonably portable. The real problems of jump designs are that certain desirable features are often contradictory. For instance, the scale jump could well be designed to be lightweight, easily transportable, and very quickly erected. A good scale jump, however, needs to be extremely strong and durable, and it is very difficult to design the scale so that all of these points are compatible. The drawings shown in Figures 8 and 9 are based upon designs by Mr P. B. Jenkins of Southampton, who, after building several sets, arrived at designs which are an excellent compromise of all the necessary features of jumping equipment. While the

Teaching the dog to scale

The scale jump perfected

The long jump – elementary lessons

The long jump – nine feet, the result of patient training

The long jump. Note the height of the dog

The clear jump

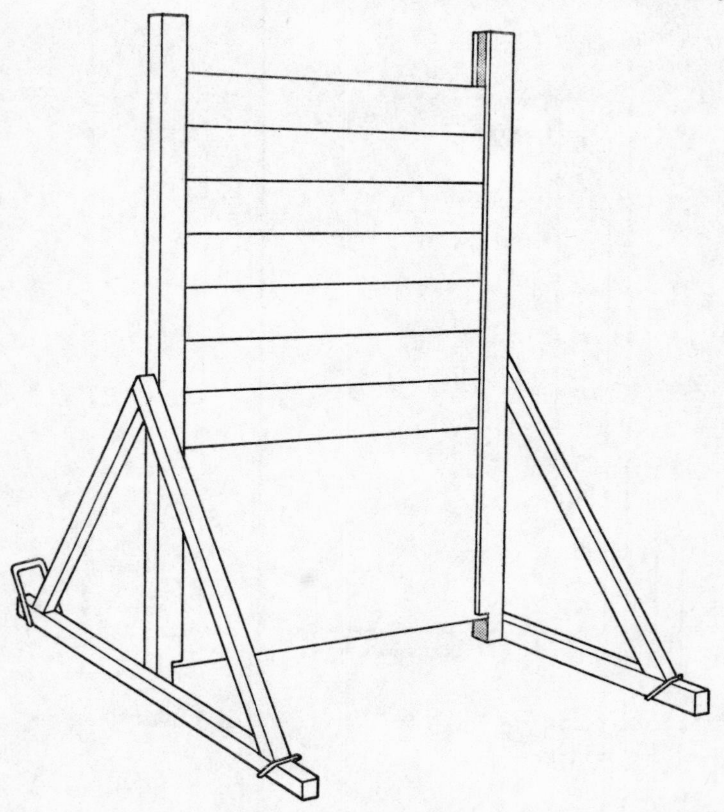

Fig. 8 Scale jump

reader might wish to arrive at his own design, these drawings show basic construction and proportion.

The design of the clear jump should take into account the three heights specified in the Kennel Club Working Trial Regulations, and for choice, it should be designed so that it is adaptable for training both the learner jumper and the experienced dog. For the learner dog, the height of the jump will need to be quite low, and as the dog progresses and the height of the top bar is raised, additional bars can be fixed to the jump. The dog experienced at the three-foot clear jump also has to be trained to jump a solitary top bar, although it would be possible for him to run underneath. It is therefore necessary to be able to remove all bars.

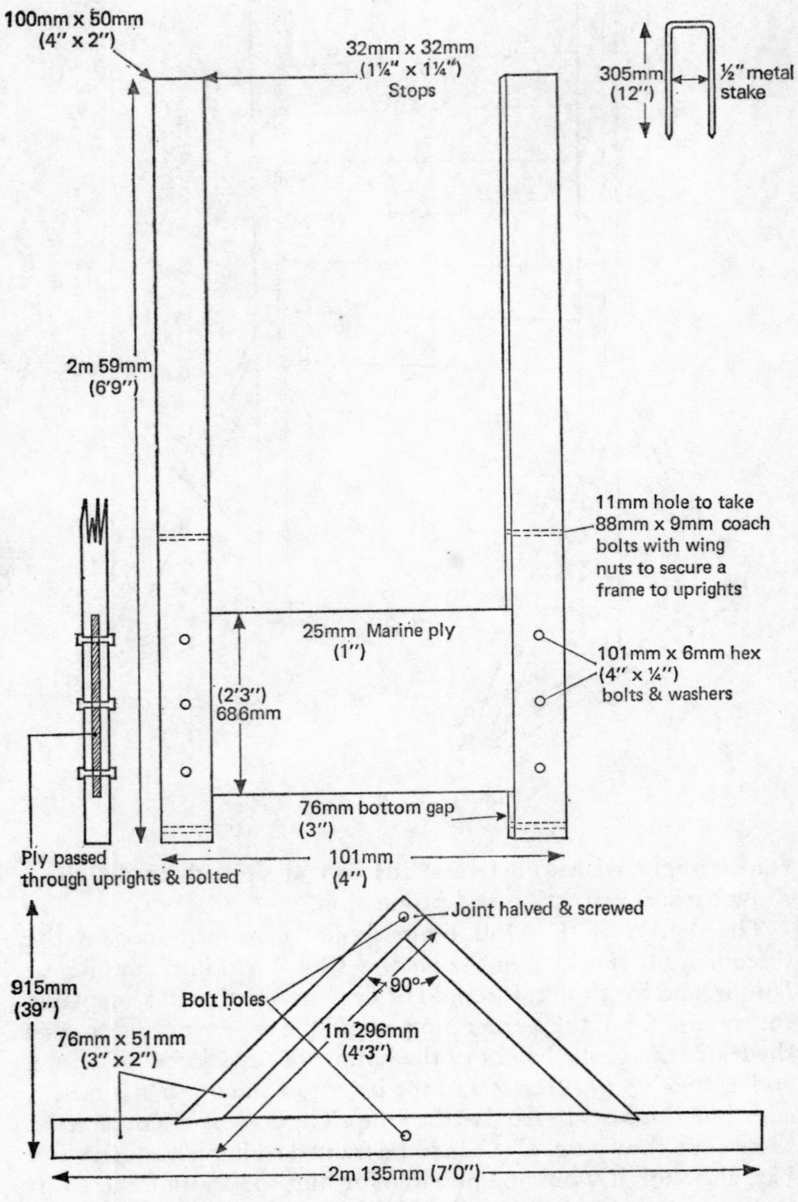

Fig. 9 Scale jump, showing construction
(The ½" metal stake should be staked to the ground)

The clear jump shown in Figure 10 is designed so that the cross bars can be rested at 3 inch intervals starting at a minimum of 1 foot, thus making it ideal for a training class where dogs might well be at different stages of training and the height of the jump needs to be altered quickly and frequently. To facilitate the three

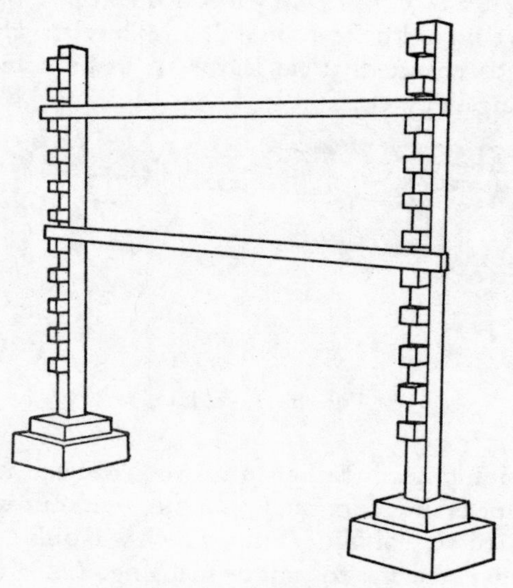

Fig. 10 Clear jump

statutory jumping heights as defined in the Working Trial Regulations, the appropriate resting blocks are painted in a different colour to the others. The base can be weighted to ensure extra stability of the upright. This jump is comprised of five pieces: two uprights and three crossbars, is easily transportable and erected in a matter of seconds.

The long jump (Figure 11) is usually made up of five or six slats increasing in height from front to back. These slats are set at an angle so that from a dog's height the slats look like one continuous expanse of obstacle. This jump is best constructed so that the rear slat is the widest at between 4 feet and 4 feet 6 inches, and its highest point is approximately 11 to 12 inches. Each slat should be progressively narrower and lower so that the front slat will be approximately 3 feet 6 inches to 4 feet wide, and the highest point will be 7 to 8½ inches. By making each slat smaller they will fit inside one another which makes them easier to store or transport. The wood to be used needs to be $\frac{3}{4}$ to 1 inch thick with the joint being glued and screwed. There is no predetermined angle at which the slats should be set, this being purely a matter of preference. The suggested heights for the slats are also a matter of choice. They can be considerably lower than those specified here, but my advice would be to train a dog on a relatively high set of long jumps to ensure that he learns to make sufficient height whilst jumping in practice.

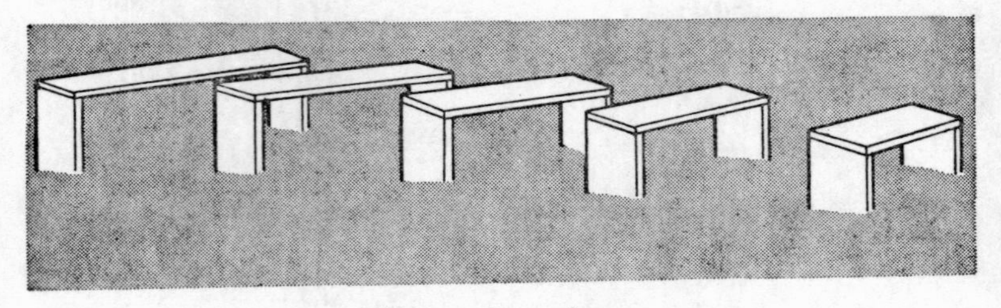

Fig. 11 Long jump

The scale jump needs to be sturdily constructed to ensure that it is capable of taking continual pounding without weakening. A dog will not trust a wobbling jump, which will only add additional apprehension problems to agility teaching. Once a scale jump has been constructed it will require four metal stakes, either of right-angle or inverted 'U' design. These stakes should be at least 10 inches long so that they can be driven into the ground to hold the jump firmly in position. The framework of the scale can be of metal or wood with the upright forming a channel to hold the boards. These boards should be 6 inches deep and $\frac{3}{4}$ to 1 inch thick, and approximately 4 feet wide. There needs to be a method of securing either one large, or several 6 inch wide boards, to the upright to obviate the necessity of cross-bracing.

The scale jump shown in Figures 8 and 9 has a simplicity of design and the frame consists of three parts which can be erected easily by one person by the use of just four bolts and wing nuts. It is also very strong and durable, and being constructed entirely of wood, should be within the scope of any handyman. The framework is two 4×2 inch uprights with $1\frac{1}{4} \times 1\frac{1}{4}$ inch stops screwed on to it. These two uprights are held rigidly together by a sheet of 1 inch marine ply let into the uprights and screwed in three places on either side starting 3 inches above the ground. This gives a minimum practice height of 2 feet 6 inches for small breeds of dog. The other pieces of the framework are two 'A' frames, 7 feet by 3 feet 3 inches, constructed from 3 × 2 inch prepared timber. The apex of the 'A' frame has a halved, screwed and glued joint, and the bottom part is slightly let into the base section. ⅜ inch coach bolts with wing nuts and washers secure the 'A' frame to the uprights at the apex and the centre of the base. The boards are 6 inches deep with three of them having a light batten affixed to either side, and the top board is padded.

For weather protection, it is better to treat the jumps with a wood preservative and, whilst it is acceptable to paint the clear and long jumps, it is infinitely better to use sawn treated boards for the scale jump to save the possibility of the dog slipping on a smooth painted surface on a wet day.

Finally on the subject of equipment, it must be mentioned that the handler will need a good set of waterproofs and wellington boots. Clothing that is just shower-proof is a poor investment; to stay dry at a Trial where it rains all day long, it pays to buy the best.

6

Competing at a Working Trial

There are many pitfalls which the hardened Trials competitor learns to avoid and which the novice falls into because of inexperience. This chapter, I hope, will provide those few tips which will help the newcomer work the dog to his best advantage and possibly save the unnecessary loss of marks.

For the purpose of this book we will assume that you are now ready to enter your first Working Trial and that you are starting your competitive life with the CD Stake. Having chosen the Trial you wish to enter and posted your entry and fee to the secretary, note carefully any special provisions that appear in the schedule with regard to the time and place that you should attend, and plan your journey carefully so that you arrive with sufficient time in hand for the dog to be exercised and carry out natural functions. However, before exercising the dog it is as well to ascertain the area in which you and your dog will be tested, and if possible keep the dog well away from it. Such action can avoid unnecessary association of ideas in what can later become the judging area and where you will be asked to carry out the send-away exercise. If, whilst exercising the dog he takes a liking to a piece of land adjacent to the eventual sendaway, you may find that whilst under test he prefers to return to this spot rather than go in the direction both you and the judge wish him to. Take the opportunity to watch one or two of the other competitors working so that you gain an idea of what will be required of you and your dog when your turn comes.

Over the years I have been asked by handlers who are new to the sport what is and is not permissible in the control and agility exercises. Such questions as 'Can I give extra commands?' are frequently asked. Every judge has his own opinions of what constitutes the perfect test, and to generalize is somewhat tricky. However, to give the beginner an idea of how he can gather as many points as possible, a rough guide to each exercise follows:

Heelwork

The dog will be expected to walk close to your left-hand side without impeding the movement of your left leg and without being too far forward or lagging behind. In the CD Stake, heelwork is tested with and without the lead attached. Whilst the dog is on the lead, the judge will expect the lead to remain slack throughout the exercise and will take into account a tight lead or any jerking of the lead when marking the exercise. If the dog is not working as you know it can, it may be preferable, and indeed save marks, to give a correction with the lead for it may result in less marks being lost as opposed to the dog that is not under control throughout the whole of the exercise. The same applies with extra commands, if it means that you will be able to get the dog under control by giving an extra command, then do so. No doubt the extra commands will be taken into account by the judge, but such vocal correction could save marks in the long run.

Sit and down

Your dog is expected to remain in these positions without moving for the time specified in the rules. Obviously, when setting up the dog you should ensure that he is comfortable, and you will be given ample time to do so. Should the dog move out of line you can expect to lose all your marks for that exercise. If he changes his position from the sit to the down or vice versa, but remains in the line, most judges will still deduct all marks.

The number of dogs that move during the stay exercises, particularly in the lower stakes, is quite alarming. If a careful study is made of the minimum number of marks that qualify a dog in the group that contains the stays, it will be seen that a handler cannot afford to lose ten marks on either of these exercises. Therefore careful training is essential.

Extra commands during the stay will usually mean the loss of all ten marks, therefore after the instructions 'Last commands', no further command or signal should be given until the exercise has finished.

Recall to handler

In this exercise you are likely to be judged on the following basis:

1 Your dog remains in the sit or down until you are ordered to call him to you.
2 He returns at a smart happy pace and shows no sign of apprehension to rejoin his handler.
3 He sits reasonably straight and speedily in front of you without command or assistance and without the handler moving his position.
4 He goes smartly to heel on your command when told to do so and not before. Once again extra commands are likely to be penalized, but they would be advisable if they speed the return of a lethargic dog or one that will not come at all on one command.

Sending the dog away

This is, as indicated previously, one of the most difficult control exercises to perfect. In the CD Stake you are likely to be given quite a straightforward sendaway of about twenty to fifty yard-length to a given area. The dog can be lined up with the given area, and most judges will allow you to send him in your own times Generally speaking, judges will be more impressed with your ability to get your dog to the given point by using extra commands if necessary, rather than a dog who either does not go anywhere near the full distance or one that finishes up in some other direc. tion. Obviously a full mark sendaway is the dog that can be sent to the exact place on one command without anticipating that command, and does so happily and not under duress.

Retrieve a dumb-bell

With the dog sitting at heel, having been given the instruction to throw your dumb-bell, try and throw it straight. The dog should not move until ordered to do so, and when he does he should move smartly out, pick up the dumb-bell cleanly, and return smartly to the present position. He should not drop the dumb-bell and you should be able to take it from him when asked to do so without any command such as 'Leave' being necessary. You will then be asked to send your dog to the heel position.

A carefully thrown dumb-bell of the correct size for the dog will help the dog rather than a wild throw that lands anywhere with a dumb-bell that the dog has difficulty in picking up. White painted ends to the dumb-bell can also be of assistance to the dog, particularly if the work is being carried out on ground where the dog may have difficulty in marking the exact position in which it fell. If your dog can execute the retrieve without extra commands it is to your advantage, but again it will probably cost you less marks to give one or more successful commands than to have the dog make a real mess of the exercise. Most judges will not be impressed with an unwilling lethargic retrieve even though the dog completes the exercise.

Elementary search

There are now twenty marks for this exercise and if you fail it completely your dog will not qualify. Many dogs do fail the search in the CD Stake and it is quite unnecessary with a dog that likes to retrieve providing that he has been taught correctly.

The handler will be shown a fifteen-yard square described by four poles, and this square will contain three different articles provided by the judge. First of all, check the wind direction and send the dog into the area from the side that enables him to work into the wind. It is permissible for the handler to walk anywhere outside of the four poles whilst the dog is working, but the handler must not step inside. You are also allowed to direct your dog without penalty whilst he is working, unless the judge feels that your commands are unnecessarily excessive and are more of a hindrance than a help to the dog. He may also deduct marks when the dog fails to obey your instructions. The great point to bear in mind is that in the exercises I have discussed so far, the dog has relied entirely upon the handler for instructions, but for the first time you are going to rely just as much upon the dog to tell you where the article is and now you and the dog must be a partnership. By the time you have entered your first Trial you should know your dog sufficiently well to understand his indication of an article and therefore know whether at this moment a little encouragement to retrieve it will be helpful. There is no need to worry about extra commands, but to please most judges, make sure those that you give are obeyed, and do not give unnecessary or excessive commands that have the effect of distracting the dog from his job.

Scale jump

In all stakes the scale jump comes first, and you will be asked whether your dog will adopt the sit, stand, or down position after being sent over and before he is ordered to return. The dog is expected to take the nominated position when you give the command to do so. Some judges will be most insistent that you start the dog from a certain point, others will not. You can be sure that once the dog has been sent over and adopted the chosen position, there will be a pause to ensure that your dog is steady before you are ordered to recall him. You should not physically help the dog over. If possible you should only give three commands. One to send him over, a second command for the dog to adopt the chosen position, and a third to recall him. However, rather than let him fail any part of the exercise, extra commands, even if penalized, would be preferable. Many judges will allow you to show the dog the jump as long as whilst you are doing so he does not make an attempt to scale. If a second attempt is necessary the dog will be penalized by 50 per cent of the marks allowed to that part of the exercise, and many judges consider a second command to send or recall as being a second attempt.

Clear jump and long jump

Both of these exercises can usually be attempted in your own time and from a position of your own choice. Once the dog has cleared the jump give him another command to drop, sit or stand to ensure that he remains steady and does not run about. You then rejoin him on the other side. Again some judges will allow you to show the dog the jump, and most will grant a second attempt should he fail the first.

Whilst many of the exercises mentioned in this chapter so far are also included in the more advanced stakes, the reader who is about to contemplate entering CD for the first time may welcome a summary.

1 Don't let the dog get bored before you are asked to work him.
2 Try and ensure that he works happily and not under duress.

3 During normal heelwork, work the dog at a smart pace and don't wait for him if he lags behind.
4 By all means give extra commands if you think that by doing so you will lose less marks, but expect to be penalized for it.
5 Do not give any extra commands or signals during the two stay exercises.
6 If you are unsure of what the judge requires, ask rather than take a chance.

Competitive tracking

At some stage or other you may decide to try your luck at an open UD Stake which is the first stake to include a track. Ensure that you arrive at the tracking base in good time to excerise, refresh, and relax your dog. Be sure to report to the base steward immediately, even though your official reporting time is not yet due. This can help the Trials management to keep things moving for they may well ask you to track earlier than originally planned.

Do not take too much notice of the alarming tales that other competitors might tell you about the track or the articles, for they are often pulling your leg or exaggerating. It is as well to check your tracking line and harness before you leave the base, making sure that they are not in a tangle.

When you arrive at the tracking area and meet the judge, be prepared to give the following details to the judge. Your name, the dog's catalogue name, and your dog's catalogue number. Listen carefully to any instructions that the judge may give you which will usually include the time allowed for completion of the track. Once you have been given those instructions, take the dog to a point about ten to fifteen yards from the pole and put the harness and line on him and see if he will pick up the track prior to reaching the starting pole.

Your track will be thirty minutes old with one article left at the end, which, although you may find that it is larger, you should assume that it will not be any bigger than a matchbox. There will be a second pole thirty yards from the start pole to indicate the direction of the first leg, but after that you and your dog are on your own. If at any time you are certain that the dog has lost the track you may, at your own discretion, take the dog back to the point at which you were certain that he was still correct and cast him again. The judge will penalize this re-cast, but if successful it would be preferable and might help you and the dog to complete the track. It is not necessary for your dog to retrieve the article. Providing that the judge is satisfied that the dog indicated it and that the handler then recovered the article, he will probably give you full marks. Once you have the article, hold up your arm to indicate to the judge, who will signify that you have finished.

Try and ensure that you car is not left in such a position that should the dog see it whilst tracking he will want to return to it. I have seen many cases of experienced and inexperienced dogs pretending to track whilst they drew their handlers back to the car.

It may be that you will overhear other competitors discussing the track pattern, or you may inadvertently see someone else tracking. If this happens, erase from your mind any preconceived ideas of the track that you may have, for never was the saying 'a little knowledge is dangerous' more true than with competitive tracking. If you allow yourself to fall into this trap you may decide that you know better than the dog and pull him off track when in fact he is right. The results of such action will be the loss of marks, but far worse, it is bad training and will only add to the dog's future confusion.

Search

The UD search and for that matter all stakes other than the CD consists of four poles describing a twenty-five-yard square. There will be four articles provided by the judge, handled and placed in the square by the search steward. Five minutes are allowed for completion of the exercise, and the judge will advise when the time starts. Make a careful note of the wind direction and send the dog from the side of the square which will allow him to work into the wind. You can command and direct your dog as required, and indeed seven marks are allotted for style and control and seven marks for each article. This is sometimes interpreted as the handler's control of the dog and the style of the dog. To take an extreme example, a judge would not be impressed by a dog that ignored all the handler's directions, continually ran out of the square and gave an appearance of not working whilst in the square. A dog such as this would most likely receive nil for style and control, and would be highly unlikely to recover any articles at all. The opposite would be the dog who is handled with the minimum amount of fuss but obeys instantly any directions, and works all the time in a happy manner whilst recovering four articles cleanly and efficiently. In this instance it would be difficult for a judge to allot anything other than full marks.

Steadiness to gunshot

This exercise is to be found in all stakes other than CD and carries a maximum of five marks. The judge, for convenience, usually tests each dog individually after the search exercise. The most common method being that the dog is walked at heelfree and as he passes the judge, or just after passing, the gun is fired once or twice. Occasionally judges will fire the gun at the completion of the search whilst the dog is running free.

The two main points the judge looks for are a lack of apprehension, although the dog is expected to take note that the gun has been fired. If he bolts in fear then five marks will be lost. There is the opposite to the gun nervous dog who will attack the person who fires the gun, again a bad and dangerous fault. This is usually only found with some dogs that have been taught criminal work where the dog associates gunfire with the possibility of being asked to bite. The wise judge sets this test very carefully as there have been cases of bitten judges. I remember well a Trial some years ago where the judge, at his previous judging appointment, had been bitten by a dog during this test, and did not want a reccurence. He therefore arranged for a steward to fire the gun, but being a decent fellow, he was also concerned for the steward's safety. The steward was therefore placed in a parked car and, as the handler and dog walked by, the window of the car was unwound, the gun quickly fired and even more speedily withdrawn, and the window rewound.

The calibre of the gun used can be anything from a ·22 starting pistol to a ·45 Colt, and I have known shotguns to be used. All these weapons have different sounds, and wise is the handler who has ensured that his dog is steady to the noise produced by most types of gun.

So far no mention has been made of the Police Dog Stake. The only difference with this stake from the others is that it includes an additional group of exercises under the heading of *patrol group*. These exercises test the dog's ability on criminal work and I have purposefully avoided any reference to training methods. Whilst I have in the past trained and qualified a dog 'Police Dog Excellent' and am not opposed to civilian handlers taking part in this event, in my opinion training methods should not be taught by the book. Any handler contemplating teaching his dog criminal work should realize the responsibilities involved. If one accepts that a dog of good temperament correctly trained for criminal work is a lethal weapon, a dog of poor temperament, wrongly trained defies description.

I cannot over-stress my convictions that this type of work should only be taught by someone of vast experience and not a person who just professes to have experience. Such a person should have the recommendation of several experienced handlers and should have the ability to assess correctly not only the dog's temperament, but also whether the prospective handler is a suitable person to be given this information.

Many owners of large breeds kept as pets proudly boast of how fierce their dog is. When this is true it is usually an indication that this type of dog is most unsuitable for criminal work. Whilst a bold type of dog is a necessary basic ingredient, it is also important that the dog should have a friendly nature and what is described as a sound temperament. Once trained for criminal work the dog should only become aggressive on command, the handler having the ability to switch the dog on and off at will.

Criminal work is an involved subject, but best left to the police or those civilians who are genuine experts in this field. Unless absolutely certain that you have the right instruction do not attempt any training.

7

Organizing a Working Trial

Working Trials are extremely complex events with many pitfalls for the inexperienced organizer. Whilst some readers may never be called upon to undertake such a task, this chapter will, I hope, show the amount of organization necessary when attempting to run an efficient Trial. As a competitor, never be too quick to criticize some small oversight or error by the promoting society, for the majority of Trial societies do the best they can with the limited number of helpers available. Most championship Trials are three-day events and as economics do not allow room for payment, helpers are either volunteers or those pressed to give of their own valuable time for the benefit of others.

The suggestions put forward here are meant as a guide as to what can be done to help a trial run smoothly, but it must be realized that to organize completely on these lines requires a large team of helpers, some of whom would not be doing very rewarding jobs. Whilst I do not wish the reader to think that the following is the only way a Trial can be operated, I have obviously tried to cover every aspect of the organization.

Trials can be run effectively by a few people, and by the same token they can be inefficient with a large body of people who do not work as a team co-ordinated by one or two experienced hands.

I have heard it said that it is unnecessary to cosset competitors and that it was never done in the old days, but time marches on and just as people of today demand labour-saving gadgets, a better standard of living and service, so the average modern Trials competitor expects a fair crack of the whip and the organization to have a professional touch about it. This surely is their right, they have paid good money to enter and may have taken time off from work to do so. They may also have travelled hundreds of miles to the venue which is another expense. So, as with the law, not only must justice be done, but it must also be seen to be done, and therefore the promoters should, as far as possible, ensure that each competitor has the same chance to triumph or fail.

I have endeavoured to deal with each duty separately as though one individual will execute that duty and nothing else, but in many cases it is possible for one person to undertake more than one job, and indeed for various reasons this is often the case. One task that is a collective operation is the committee, and as a Trial is born in committee, we will start here.

THE COMMITTEE

If the Trial is a new venture then the first decision must be whether sufficient tracking land is available, and approximately how many entries are likely to be received. This latter point can always be gauged by entries received at similar Trials in that part of the country.

Whilst it is permissible to limit entries to not less than thirty dogs per stake for any stake other than that which carries the Working Trial Certificate, if at all possible a new Trial should avoid limitation. Without doubt the majority of Trials competitors are anti-limitation, and to become established a society needs the goodwill of the competitors. I do not like to see limitation, but one must accept that land and people's time become increasingly scarce, and limited entry Trials must be better than no Trials at all.

The date of the event and the stakes that are to be scheduled are committee decisions. Obviously a date to be avoided is one already used by another society that is likely to effect your entry, and the number of stakes scheduled will depend on land and the help available.

Judges must be appointed, and whilst only championship Trial judges have to be approved by the Kennel Club, it is wise for the newer society to seek the services of established judges. It must be realized that the further away from the venue the judges live, the higher the expense of bringing them to the Trial. They will need to be accommodated from the night before the first tracking day to the end of the Trial, and possibly a further night if any great distance exists between the venue and their home.

One of the most important duties is that of catering. At the control and agility venue, either a firm of caterers can be appointed, or the society can manage their own catering. If the latter is the case, then it is wise to appoint a catering manageress who will gather around her a team of ladies to prepare and dispense the food on required days. Someone once said that an army marches on its stomach, and if that is so, track-layers, search stewards and judges are an army who need to be sustained throughout each very long day. Sometimes it is possible for a lunch break to be worked into the tracking schedule with the judges returning to a control point for a sit-down hot or cold meal. On the other hand, if the entries mean continuous judging, then each member of the team will need a packed lunch and liquid refreshment, which is best handed to them at the start of the day so that they can choose their own time to eat.

At many Trials the track-layers have to be out at daybreak, which can be 5 a.m. and if this is the case, a packed breakfast that arrives at 7 or 8 o'clock is very acceptable. Whatever happens, ensure that the nosework team want for nothing in the way of refreshment. You can be sure that they will appreciate it and will be more likely to help again at the next Trial.

If the society has sufficient experienced people available then the committee can ease the organization burden of the secretary by appointing people to carry out specific duties during the Trial as follows:

Secretary, plus assistant secretary
Trial manager
Tracking steward
Obedience steward

The secretary

The first job of the secretary is to apply to the Kennel Club for permission to hold a Trial. Such application should state which stakes it is intended to schedule and the proposed dates. The Kennel Club will then send the official application form stating the date granted to the society. This form, the licence, must be completed and returned to the Kennel Club together with two draft copies of the schedule, the names of the judges and a specimen entry form at least sixty days prior to the date of the proposed Trial. Although this will comply with Kennel Club Regulations, sixty days is leaving matters a little late, and the wise secretary will carry out this job several months before the Trial. It should also be remembered that until the licence has been granted by the Kennel Club the date will not be published in the Kennel Gazette Trials Guide. Before the draft schedule is sent to the Kennel Club, the committee should have approved it, which, in the case of an established society, will prove to be something of a formality.

The committee should give a considerable amount of thought to the schedule, with particular reference being made to any innovations that are slightly different from the accepted way of running Trials. For example, it is extremely helpful to the office on the final day, if the CD stays have been carried out well before the end of the CD judging, for until the stays have been judged it is impossible for the office to write certificates and determine the results.

A map shown in the schedule of the vicinity in which the trials are being held can be of great assistance to the new competitor, and if signposts are also being used, it is helpful for the map to show where the signs commence.

The judges should also have been invited by the committee and acceptance received, the initial approach to the judge having been made by the secretary at least twelve months in advance, or it may be found that they are already committed to judge elsewhere.

Printing of the schedule and entry forms should be arranged so that they can be posted to prospective competitors three to four weeks prior to the date of closing entries, with at least a month allowed for printing and delivery as printers can be notoriously long-winded.

Although some judges provide their own judging sheets, the secretary should have a stock of two judging sheets for each stake: one which will be used by the judge whilst testing the nosework group and steadiness to gunshot and allows sufficient room for the track pattern to be drawn, and the other which shows all the remaining exercises and includes the total nosework and gunshot marks. The maximum number of points plus the minimum group qualifying marks should also be shown on this sheet. If more than one stake is being held it is extremely helpful for identification purposes if these judging sheets are printed on a different colour for each stake. On the final day of the trial where four different stakes are being held and judging sheets from all four stakes are continuously arriving at the office, this colour code is a great help to a possibly harassed secretary.

Prize cards and rosettes need to be ordered well in advance, as do qualifying certificates or certificates of merit. The rules of the Kennel Club Working Trials Regulations (S.1) give clear instructions as to the wording required. Office score sheets for each stake, and preferably a duplicate set which can be prominently displayed for the competitors' benefit, need to be obtained or drawn. As the question of whether or not a dog has qualified is to the inexperienced a complicated procedure, much thought should be given to the format of the score sheets. An example of a score sheet which shows immediately if a dog is qualifying, is shown on the following page, and the reader will notice that the bottom section is a group total column. If a red pen is used to mark the total marks for dogs qualifying in that group, and a blue or black pen used for the dogs that fail a group of exercises and fail overall, the exact position can then be seen at a glance.

Once the entry is known, the tracking steward and Trial manager should be consulted as to how they wish to plan the tracking, i.e. the number of tracks per stake per day, the interval between each dog, and reporting time for each handler. These are decisions of importance, and a guide to how the answer should be reached is shown under the heading 'The tracking steward'.

When the secretary has been given the timetable it is necessary to advise each competitor of the time they are required to report at base. If justice is done, it is advisable that a minimum number of people know which dogs are due to report at any given time, and it should not be necessary for more than the secretary and Trial manager to be in possession of these facts. Therefore, all that need be stated to each competitor is the time they are to report at base and if a further draw will be made at that time. A way of ensuring that justice is done is for competitors to be given a reporting time only in groups of three. If only the Trial manager and secretary are in possession of the list of dogs due to report, and the tracking steward and his track-layers are not, a further draw can be made at the reporting time to determine the order in which the three handlers and dogs work. Thus there is no sus-

A typical score sheet

CONTROL

TD	No.	62	47	87	22	10	33	57
Heelfree	5	4½	4	4½	5	4	4	4
Sendaway	10	5	6½	7	9½	4½	3	2
Speak	5	4½	0	2½	3	5	5	0
Down	10	10	10	10	10	10	10	10
Gunshot	5	5	5	5	5	5	5	5

AGILITY

Scale	10	10	9½	10	10	9½	10	9
Clear	5	5	5	5	5	5	5	5
Long	5	5	2½	5	5	5	5	2½

NOSEWORK

Search	35	35	35	35	35	27	16	27
Track	100	96	97	98	95	12	99	92

GROUP TOTALS

Articles	30	20	10	30	30	10	10	0
Control	35/25	**29**	**25½**	**29**	**32½**	**28½**	**27**	21
Agility	20/14	**20**	**17**	**20**	**20**	**19½**	**20**	**16½**
Nosework	165/116	**151**	**142**	**163**	**160**	*49*	**125**	**119**
Total	220	**200**	**184½**	**212**	**212½**	97	**172**	**156½**
70%	155						*	
80%	176	*	*	*	*			
Place		3rd		2nd	1st			

NOTE: Each group total should be shown in red (bold above) where the dog has qualified, and in black where he has failed.

picion of track-layers laying good or bad tracks for a particular dog as they will not know which dog is due to track until it arrives at the starting pole.

It is also extremely helpful if this advice of tracking time contains a map of the area immediate to the base, and where signposts showing the route to the Trials commence. A map and these details may have been included in the schedule, but if no further costs are to be incurred then it does no harm for them to be repeated.

Another point that should not be overlooked is that permission to use both the tracking land and the obedience venue should have been obtained from the owners. At some stage prior to the event it will be necessary to arrange accommodation for the judges. It may well be that some of the members are prepared to offer accommodation, and no doubt this would be discussed in committee. If such an arrangement is not possible, then hotels must be contacted, and according to local conditions, an early booking might be necessary. If it is envisaged that many of the competitors will congregate at a certain hotel in the evenings, then this is the ideal place for the judges to stay. Judges are just as interested as competitors in chatting about dogs in general and it makes the event more sociable for them if they can mix in the evenings with people who share the same interest. Over a period of weeks, and months prior to the event, the secretary will have completed the major part of the work, and, until the final day, can afford to relax a little, unless other duties such as base steward have been undertaken. Whilst tracking is taking place, all that is necessary is to keep both the official and competitors' score sheets up to date, and in all probability answer the frequent queries from competitors. The final day of the Trials is now the secretary's immediate problem, and listed below are the important items that must be available.

Trophies
Prize cards
Rosettes
Prize money
Qualifying certificates
Ring numbers
Score sheets

There may be many other items to be taken on the final day, such as raffle tickets and prizes, pens, pencils, paper, drawing pins, etc., but the above are the essential items that cannot be forgotten.

During the afternoon life becomes hectic and it is advisable that the secretary has an assistant who, for preference, will be conversant with determining those who have qualified. Both sets of score sheets need to be kept up to date during this period, and as each competitor completes their work the totals have to be added, double-checked and qualifiers noted. It is at this stage that a well laid out score sheet showing qualifiers in each group in a different coloured pen becomes invaluable. Qualifying certificates have to be neatly written and everything put in an easily identifiable order prior to the prize giving. It is essential that the secretary and assistant are not interrupted for other than essential questions at this stage, and competitors should always remember to keep well away from them so that the work can be completed with a minimum of delay.

Tracking steward

This job must be undertaken by a person with a vast experience of track-laying problems and a flair for organization. Someone has to ascertain that sufficient tracking land is available before a decision to hold the Trial is taken, and this task is usually undertaken by the tracking steward and the Trial manager or other experienced people. In the case of established events it is something of a formality, with the secretary applying for permission to lay tracks on land that has been used in the past.

Once the total number of entries is known the tracking steward and the Trial manager should confer to decide on the best system and timetable for tracking, and they should take into account the distance between each piece of land to be used. For instance, it is normal practice for a judge to allow twenty minutes for the completion of a track, a minimum of a further ten minutes is necessary to allow sufficient time for the handler and the dog to complete the five-minute search exercise and steadiness to gunshot test. This then means that the minimum interval between each dog is thirty minutes, and this is only possible where the next track can be reached by the judge within two minutes. This interval between dogs is generally only used when the society has a large entry to cater for, and although with careful planning and a team of experienced people it is quite possible to keep rigidly to the thirty-minute timetable, it is preferable to allow a further five or ten minutes between each dog. The whole point is that whatever timetable is decided upon, the society must be capable of keeping to it barring unforeseen circumstances, and the intervals between each dog must take into account the time taken for the judge to get to the next track.

There are many variations in the order of timing of the nose-work tests, and experience tells the tracking steward which one is most suitable to the land, the number of dogs to be worked and the amount of daylight hours available. For example, the normal system is for the dog to work the track then carry out the search followed by the gunshot test. Some variations are:

1 A number of searches followed by the same number of tracks.
2 Two tracks followed by two searches.
3 Dog 'A' to track followed by Dog 'B' to track, followed by Dog 'A' to search. (This system allows a rest for each dog between track and search.)
4 Four tracks followed by four searches.

Once the tracking steward has decided how many dogs can be scheduled for nosework on each day (taking into consideration spare time and spare land being available at the end of the day, to cater for unforseen circumstances), he should then draw up a timetable such as the one shown on page 116. This allows him to see at a glance when any given track-layer will be free to lay again, and the number of tracks that can be laid in succession by that person, allowing him to report back to the judge in time for judging the first track of the group.

Having drawn up a timetable it will be possible to see whether the track-layers are going to lay tracks in batches of one, two, three, four, five or six. For example, if Joe lays the first three TD tracks and Bill lays the fourth, fifth and sixth tracks, it can be seen at a glance that Joe, who has finished with the judge on track three, is now available to lay track seven. If not, and only two track-layers are available, then the number of consecutive tracks to be laid by one person must be altered. Once the track-layer's sequence is decided, then the tracking steward should work out the reporting time. I prefer to have at least two dogs and handlers who have reported at base at all times, apart from the next scheduled dog, although this is not necessary for the first two or three tracks early in the morning. The reason for this is that there are always cancellations after reporting times have been sent to the competitors and sometimes handlers do not arrive, having failed to notify the society that they are unable to do so. If at all possible, for the sake of good organization, a handler must go to every length to get a message to the Trial organizers that he will not be attending.

Whilst some handlers may find it inconvenient to report up to two hours before their eventual track time, with the large entries that most societies face these days, it is essential that land and time are not wasted, and having an extra two dogs at base means that dogs can be brought forward to work a track that was in fact laid for another competitor and so no wastage occurs.

A tracking steward's completed timetable for the WD stake would look like the following example:

Track number	Reporting time	Track-laying time	Track running time	Track-layer finished time	Track-layer
1	7·30	6·30	8·00	8·20	
2	7·50	7·00	8·30	8·50	Joe
3	8·20	7·30	9·00	9·20	
4	8·20	8·00	9·30	9·50	
5	8·40	8·30	10·00	10·20	Bill
6	8·50	9·00	10·30	10·50	
7	9.20	9·30	11·00	11·20	
8	9·50	10·00	11·30	11·50	Joe
9	10·20	10·30	12·00	12·20	
10	10·50	11·00	12·30	12·50	
11	11·20	11·30	1·00	1·20	Bill
12	11·50	12·00	1·30	1·50	

Note: The dog due for track four is reporting early enough to be put on track two, and that the dog scheduled to run track six would be in time to run track three.

It will also be seen that, assuming the judge allows twenty minutes for the track, each track-layer has only ten minutes from the end of his third track when he is finished with the judge until he is due to lay his next track. With this particular timetable it would be prudent to use a third track-layer if twenty tracks were to be run on that day, or else neither Joe nor Bill will get a break throughout the day, and in fact Joe will work virtually non-stop for eleven hours, laying and watching eleven tracks, and that would be too much, particularly in rough country. All these points must be taken into consideration, and whilst the timetable shown gives an indication of how timings will work out, I would not use that system with twenty dogs a day and just two track-layers.

By now the tracking steward will have a good idea of who he has available to lay the tracks. The wise steward will surround himself with reliable experienced track-layers or those he has personally taught and is satisfied that they are good enough to be let loose in competition. Beware of the person who volunteers his services but who knows nothing about the job, for it is the tracking steward's moral duty to ensure that those people laying tracks are going to give the handler a fair chance, not just by reasons of honesty, but because they know exactly what they are doing, where they have walked and where the articles are.

Most experienced competitors have at some time or another suffered from bad track-layers, and also listened to them telling the judge that some other competitor's dog is going wrong, when in fact the dog is right and it is the track-layer who has forgotten where he has been. A good judge will not be influenced by a suspect track-layer if convinced that the dog is correct, but I have seen it happen and have felt very sorry for the poor competitor who may have travelled from the other end of the country, taken a day or more away from work and paid his entry fee.

Prior to the Trial commencing, the tracking steward should have been in touch with the judge to advise him of the size of land available for each track and the type of terrain. This will enable the judge to set his track pattern and choose his articles accordingly. At the same time the judge will advise whether he will post his articles and track pattern to the tracking steward or whether he will want to meet all his track-layers the day before for briefing and hand over the pattern and articles at the same time.

In the absence of instructions from the judge, the track-layers should be detailed about the amount of scent to be put on the articles, and whether the articles are to be placed in a clearing or in heather, for it would hardly be fair for Joe to do one thing and Bill to do the other.

Preferably the tracking steward should not schedule himself to lay any tracks. This leaves him free to act in a completely supervisory capacity and as an emergency track-layer. It may well be that he is supervising the track-laying in other stakes as well, and in this case it would be virtually impossible for him to be tied down to a tracking timetable as a track-layer in either stake. His job is to make sure that the nosework runs smoothly and someone has to be available to take spot decisions about the field which should have been available but (a) now has cows in it, (b) the army have just moved in to carry out an exercise on the tracking land, (c) the track has been fouled by riders and horses. These are just a few examples of the problems and there are many more that can and do happen. One could probably write a book just on the problems of competitive track-laying alone.

Never ask a track-layer to help at the Trial and then only ask him to lay one or two tracks if he has taken time away from work to help you out. Whilst he will not want to be worked to death, he will expect to do a fair day's work.

If the tracking steward is not familiar with the land he should walk each field or land allotted for a track with his track-layers at some time prior to the event. The ground that looks good for a track from the probable starting point can hide many unknown hazards which are only found when the track is being laid, and should the track-layer be unable to continue to lay the track because of a hazard the whole timetable is ruined when, with a little thought and work before the event, that piece of land could have been left out of the schedule.

The tracking steward should be satisfied that the search steward knows what is to be done and that the judge's instructions are being carried out. Again, each dog should have as near as possible a similar piece of searching ground to the others with the same amount of scent on the articles as with the track. It becomes unfair for one dog to have the articles in deep thick heather, another dog having the articles laid in clearings.

So much for the tracking steward, which is probably the most important duty at a trial. A brief summary of his job is shown below:

1 Ascertain the number of dogs entered.
2 Get in touch with the judge (remember to ask if he will provide his own gun).
3 Advise secretary of reporting times.
4 Work out the tracking timetable.
5 Appoint the track-layers and search stewards.

6 Check the land and walk it with the track-layers if necessary, at least twenty-four hours prior to the Trial.
7 Ensure that there is a foolproof system of getting the dogs and handlers from the base to their track (see Trial manager).
8 Ensure that plenty of food and drink has been arranged for the nosework team.

The tracks at a Trial are laid under the instructions of the judge who will have briefed the tracking steward. Laying tracks, either at a Trial or in practice, requires experience and/or instruction. There are many mistakes which can be made, and it must be remembered that in competition the dog only has one chance. If the track-layer does not know his job and makes a mistake, either in laying the track or interpreting the dog's reaction on the track, then that competitor has not had a fair chance.

In theory, a good tracking dog should be able to track anywhere at any time. Of course in practice this is not always so, but Trials organizers should always try to ensure that the conditions are, as far as possible, the same for every dog. The very nature of Working Trials means that it is impossible to get any two track-layers to lay the same track, footstep for footstep, on two different pieces of land, and of course tracking held over two or three days could well have differing weather conditions. Track-laying in a field that is only large enough to take one track and has a distinct boundary such as a hedge or fence, poses less problems than track-laying in open country. For instance there is no problem of the track-layer inadvertently crossing the previous track or part of the ground allocated to the following track. In open country the track-layers have to be aware of additional problems and the judge advised very quickly should the dog stray badly off course to the extent where the next track may be interfered with. It is therefore commonsense that, where possible, the track-layers should know the land on which they are to lay tracks, and in the absence of this knowledge, the tracking steward should be able to advise them of any peculiarities of the land. Experienced track-layers know only too well that land which looks suitable when viewed from the approximate start of the track can hide all sorts of problems that are only to be found when stumbled upon – tall undergrowth which is impossible to get through, a stream too wide to jump, a sudden decline that is more like a precipice, or a fence that was not visible from the start. These are a few examples and there are many more.

So many things can go wrong and the attitude of 'say nothing, the competitor will never know' is to be deplored. If there is an error then the only acceptable one is that which is slightly in favour of the dog and handler, and other than that the track-layer should remove the starting pole and lay a fresh track elsewhere. In the absence of definite instructions from the judge, a track-layer should make up his mind how he is going to fit the pattern on the land before commencing. Having done so, place the starting pole in the ground and hold the article, or articles, in a hand and walk towards a definite marker such as a distant pylon, gap in the hedge, tree, etc. This marker should of course be suitable to the track pattern, and on each new leg of the track a suitable marker should be noted. Where possible all markers should be selected in relation to the start pole for it has to be remembered that on flat open ground this is where the track-layer and judge will view most of the track from. It is all very well selecting a marker whilst in the middle of laying the track, but is the track-layer going to be able to pinpoint that marker when standing with the judge? Markers that are obvious to the handler should be avoided. For example, an old hand at the sport will be looking for an article next to the lone tree or the water trough, etc. If such a marker is used, the article should be placed several yards before or after, but if it is that obvious, better that it is not used at all. The same applies to the position in which the article has been laid. The track-layer who can tell the judge where a turn or article is and be correct within a yard is a rare beast indeed. If slightly unsure it is far better to keep quiet for it is unlikely that the judge is a fool, he knows the pattern he has set and where the articles are likely to be, and should his track-layer say that the dog has passed the article and the dog then finds it twenty yards later, the track-layer is the one who looks a little foolish.

Consideration should be made as to where the articles are going to be laid on land with a variation in terrain. It seems to me unfair that one dog should have his article at the bottom of deep heather and another in a clearing. It is not always possible that every dog will get exactly the same type of location for the article, but some collusion between judge and track-layers can help to make the degree of difficulty more uniform.

It is good practice to make notes of turns and articles, etc., whilst laying the track. This is most advisable for new track-layers and usually necessary for the more experienced when laying three or more tracks consecutively as can happen in a TD Stake. Typical track patterns are shown in Figure 12. To ensure that extra pockets of scent are not left where the turns or articles are located, the track-layer should stop to make notes several yards after turns or articles. An experienced person learns to lay tracks in a similar manner to a good driver who, whilst being conscious of what he is doing in his immediate vicinity, is also aware of any hazards and of exactly what has to be done. Thus such a person would have selected the turning points, etc. many yards ahead.

When tracking is taking place on the same land on more than one day, the track-layer should be able to remove from the land any articles that the handlers and dogs have failed to recover. This avoids the possibility of dogs finding articles on a track, or even in the search square, that have been left from a previous day's tracking.

Good track-layers do not grow on trees and societies are rarely blessed with more than they need to run an event. It is therefore somewhat essential that experienced handlers should now and again volunteer their services as track-layers. It is possible to teach almost anyone to lay tracks, but an experienced handler should sometimes be seen to be a worker as well. Who better to teach to lay tracks than someone who knows what it is like to be on the end of a tracking line with just a pole and a dog between success and failure?

The Working Trial manager

The Working Trial manager has the overall authority for the smooth running of the event. This person should be sufficiently experienced to make on the spot decisions. He should not be a petty dictator but should delegate responsibility to the team working with him, i.e.: the secretary, the chief tracking steward and the obedience steward, each of whom will take decisions affecting their own particular job, but if necessary ask the advice of the Trial manager. Sometimes the secretary and Trial manager are one and the same person, but the ideal situation is a person who is free from all other duties and spends time ensuring the success of the Trial. The tracking steward has a full-time job from the

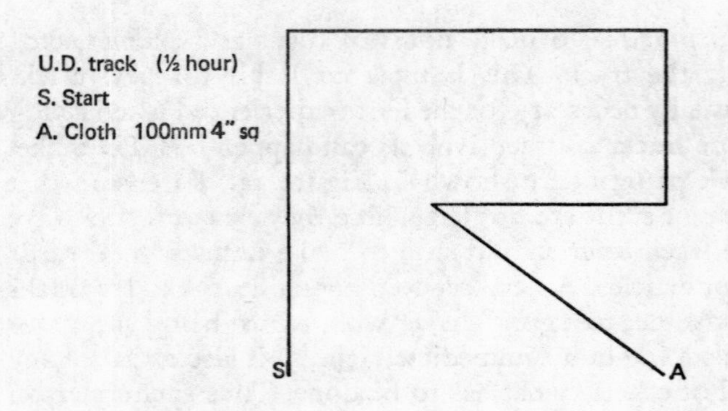

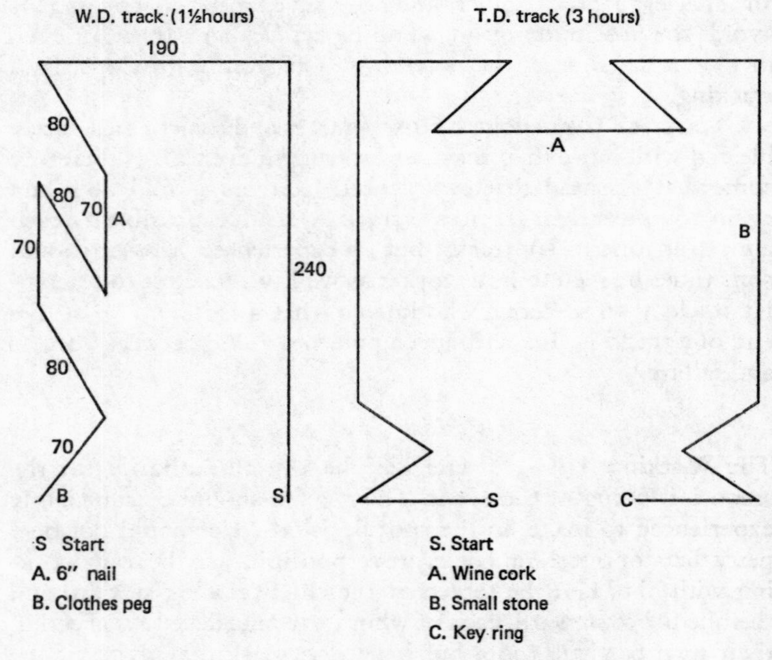

Fig. 12 Typical track patterns of 880 yards

start of tracking until it ends, so therefore it is better for the Trial manager to brief and be in control of the base steward and the people who have been detailed to escort competitors to their track. This latter job is most important if the tracking ground is spread over a very wide area, and obviously the people undertaking this duty need to know where each track is situated. They should leave the base with the competitor so that they arrive unhurried but in good enough time for the dog to be given his final exercise, etc., and if the competitor is unsure of the way to return to base, arrange to escort them back after they have finished the nosework. When the tracking land is all in one reasonably compact area, such as common land etc., a good signposting system from the base to a convenient place out of sight and just prior to the current piece of land being worked by a dog, can be successfully used instead of escorts. The point being that it does not really matter what system is used to get competitors from the base to their track as long as they arrive at their tracking land unhurried and without the worry of whether or not they are lost. Experienced competitors tend to know their way around most societies' tracking land, but it should not be forgotten that newcomers to the sport will probably be grateful for a foolproof system which gets them to the required place.

Whilst on the subject of signposting, if the trial is being held off the beaten track, then the Trial manager should ensure that signposts to the base and the control and agility venue are prominently displayed in strategic places. In actual terms of physical work, unless undertaking other duties as well, the Trial manager does not appear to have much to do, but it is a rarity to find a Trial manager kicking his heels doing nothing. There is always plenty to be done, and as his job is mainly one of co-ordination, he needs to be free to go anywhere in the Trial area at any time.

The base steward probably has the most boring task of all but one that is extremely important. An unsociable person does not make a good base steward. Very often the secretary will act in this capacity as they are well aware of who is to report and at what time. This is usually the competitors' first contact with the trials, and as the saying goes 'first impressions count', for the base steward should welcome the competitors in a cheerful manner, answer their queries, and do his best to put them at ease.

It is a good idea for the committee to have appointed a control and agility steward who should work under the direction of the Trial manager and be responsible for arranging sufficient sets of jumps to be brought to and erected at the venue. This steward should also ensure that each judge and his personal steward have everything they need throughout the day, thus relieving the secretary and/or Trial manager of unnecessary worry.

Should the Trial include a PD (Police Dog) Stake, then experienced people to act as criminals should be arranged beforehand, and sufficient protective clothing and overcoats provided, to minimize the risk of one of them being hurt. Needless to say, it is wise to have a first-aid kit handy. All this would probably fall to the lot of the Trial manager who should have sufficient experience of PD to take the right decisions.

Once again it is helpful to the office if all dogs qualifying in the PD Stake prior to the commencement of criminal work are run early during the criminal work. This would need the judge's approval, but a good idea is for two or three non-qualifying dogs to run first. These enable the judge to adjust his test if necessary before the qualifying dogs work, followed by the qualifiers so far, followed by the remainder of the non-qualifiers. This means that there will be a minimum of delay by the office before they are in a position to announce the results once judging is completed.

Elementary tracking. *Above*: Handler attracting dog's attention before placing the article. *Below*: Handler indicating the start of the track

Tracking – dog locating and retrieving an article on the track

Tracking – dog casting on a turn. The line is under control and the handler has line in reserve

The dog begins to track; the handler pays out the line from a neat coil

A result of bad line handling

The search. The dog has dropped an article just inside the area and the handler encourages the dog to retrieve it

The search. The handler has moved back from the area to take the article

8

The History of Working Trials

Working Trials in Great Britain date back to 1924 when, on 30 January, the Alsatian Sheep Police & Army Dog Society (ASPADS) held the first event. This society later dropped the word 'Alsatian' from their title, substituting 'Associated' in its place, for originally only Alsatians competed.

The Alsatian League and Club of Great Britain also started Trials, and they were in fact, the first club to hold a Championship Working Trial recognized by the Kennel Club. This event took place at Castle Bromwich during May 1927. They only held a total of six Championship Trials before giving up the sport in 1934. The ASPADS continued to pioneer Working Trials, and by tradition still hold more Trials per year than any other society. The Kennel Club rules of those early days of Trials were for Alsatian Wolf Dogs, as they were then known in this country, and were those rules agreed upon by the ASPADS and the League.

The Working Trial enthusiast has to accept all kinds of weather, and to call some of the prevailing Trials weather conditions inclement, would at times be using a very kind word. It is therefore interesting to note that the judge of that very first Trial stated in his report that 'dense banks of fog obscured everything beyond a radius of fifteen yards'.

One of the most prolific winners during the first eight years of championship events was Miss Jean Workman who imported several highly trained Alsatians from Germany and competed with them in England with a large degree of success. The competitors in those days were usually those of sufficient financial means to devote the necessary time to the sport, indeed the judge would often be supplied with a horse and groom to enable him to carry out his duties. Considering that entries were sometimes as low as four dogs, today's judge, who might be expected to judge in excess of forty dogs over three days, would consider this to be something of a luxury. With so few people having sufficient knowledge of the sport, it was an unwritten rule, that having entered a Trial it was one's duty to act in an official capacity at the next event, and it was only in this somewhat informal manner that Trials were able to be held.

Because of the low number of entries, particularly in the Open Stake of championship events, whilst two wins made the dog a Working Trial Champion, there had to be a minimum of eight entries for one of these wins to qualify towards the title of Champion. This minimum entry rule was later rescinded but the reader should bear this in mind when reading the list of Working Trial Certificate winners in the appendix.

In those early days both organizers and competitors were learning by the hard school of experience and many peculiar things happened. For instance, at a Trial in 1929 a German judge stated that the track-layers had placed flags near to the turns on the track and near to where the articles had been laid. His conclusion, which would no doubt be echoed by today's judges, was that those flags were a help to handlers with poor dogs and a hindrance to those with good dogs.

In 1927 one of the most outstanding events in the Working Trial calendar was first held. It was known as the North versus South match and was held annually until the early 1960s. The dogs were tested on more control and agility exercises than were scheduled for a normal trial, in fact scent discrimination was one of the additional tests. Handlers and dogs, in teams of five, competed for a total of 680 points and a challenge cup went to the winning team, with a gold medal for the best individual performance.

The Working Trial tests scheduled by a society up until the alteration of the rules in 1961 were Junior Stakes, this was the beginning test from which the Companion Dog Stake, as we know it today, was evolved. Also, and perhaps more interesting, it was from the Junior Stakes that Obedience Competitions were taken. After Junior Stakes the progression was Senior 'B' Stakes, followed by Senior 'A' Stakes, and finally Open Stakes. The later stake being similar to today's top stake, for the dogs gained either

TD or PD qualifications according to which test was scheduled. It is interesting that apart from the six-foot scale jump, an additional test was incorporated in the stakes which required the dog to retrieve a minimum weight ten-ounce dumb-bell over the scale jump.

The Tracking Dog Open Stakes included interesting nosework tests. For instance, the leash track was approximately one mile long having been laid two hours previously. For the track 400 marks were allotted, and four different kinds of articles were dropped by the track-layer *en route*. In the regulations in force during the late fifties there was a progression of marks for each article as follows:

1st article – 20 marks
2nd article – 30 marks
3rd article – 50 marks
4th article – 75 marks

Quite obviously, with the marks for the recognition of the articles allocated progressively higher, if any were to be missed by the dog it was better that he did not fail to recognize the last two.

However, the regulations prior to these required that the track be crossed by two fresh tracks and that two articles were dropped by the track-layer, one about the middle and one at the end of the track. The track-layer was also instructed to leave an article at the commencement of the track. It seems that the regulations have never remained very stable for long. For instance, the time allotted for the search was increased from five to seven minutes in 1963, only to be reduced to five minutes again a few years later. Test number 7 was the seek back, and the regulation for this test was self-explanatory – 'The seek back shall be not less than two hundred yards, but a longer distance if available for handler's article. The article used, which must not be a conspicuous one, nor a handkerchief, to be approved by the judge. The article to be dropped surreptitiously by the handler after he has proceeded at least thirty paces.'

A free track was also included as test number 8. It was approximately 400 yards long, not necessarily in a straight line, and was a quarter of an hour old. The dog was given a heel mark of the track-layer and was then expected to identify the track-layer's article at the end of the track. Over the last thirty yards of the track other strangers' articles (similar in nature to the one left by the track-layer) were scattered as decoys. Having discriminated, the dog was expected to return to the handler with the article. The dog was awarded 75 marks for the track and 125 marks for the article discrimination. It is arguable whether today's Tracking Dog Stake schedules are a more difficult or easy nosework group than in the days prior to the early 1960s.

The first ever Obedience Show not to schedule breed classes as well was held by the Alsatian League and Club of Great Britain in October 1949 at Finchley Road Baths, London, although obedience tests had previously been scheduled at breed shows. At such a breed show during the 1930s, Captain P. L. C. Gurney and a gentleman by the name of Charlie Bates, competed in an obedience test. As far as is known this was the first ever event of its kind.

In the very early days of Working Trials it was not uncommon for the first prize to be £25. Compared with today's prize money and the comparable value of the pound, such a sum was worth winning. Today's prize money usually does not cover the cost of attending the Trial. This situation has been brought about by the ever increasing cost of holding Trials and is likely to remain with us.

The ASPADS continued to be the sole pioneers of Trials up until 1939 when the war brought a halt to such activities. They recommenced Championship Trials in 1947 with Mary Porterfield steering the society as secretary, gathering around her a number of people who were to be the backbone of the ASPADS for several years. They remained the only championship society until 1955 when the Southern Alsatian Training Society (SATS) were granted the same status by the Kennel Club. Mrs Mary Hester had recently taken over as secretary of the SATS and it was under her guidance that the society entered into Working Trials, having previously been purely a training society. However, in conjunction with the Northern Alsatian Training Society, they were responsible for holding the annual North versus South match. Since 1955 the SATS have flourished and remained a leading force in Working Trial promotion.

Two years later in 1957 the Surrey Dog Training Society were to gain championship status and with such people as Sir Joseph and Lady Simpson, Mr Ken Butler and Mr Bob Montgomery being involved, this society was quickly established at the top. In those days, whilst the entries for the certificate at Working Trials in the Surrey/Kent area would be in the region of ten, they could still be as low as four or five in other parts of the country, for with Surrey, the SATS and the ASPADS Southern Branch, this corner of England was the stronghold of Working Trials.

In 1961 the Kennel Club formed a sub-committee under the chairmanship of Sir Joseph Simpson, OBE, to revise the Working Trial Regulations. Although these regulations have been revised again, taking effect from January 1977, they are still basically those rules introduced in 1961 which have certainly stood the test of time. Sir Joseph had become the Chief Constable of Surrey in 1947 and at that time had decided to reorganize and enlarge the police dog section of his constabulary. He took a great personal interest in the dog section and encouraged his dog handlers to enter civilian Working Trials.

There is no doubt that the entry of the police into Working Trials has perhaps influenced the growth of the sport more than any other single factor. They won their first Working Trial Certificate in 1949 with a Dobermann, Ulf Von Margarethenhof, handled by Sgt Harry Darbyshire of the Surrey Constabulary, who was later awarded the British Empire Medal for his service to police dogs. Harry Darbyshire went on to make the dog up to a Working Trial Champion, and just to prove that it was no fluke, he did the same thing with two Alsatians, Loki of Hatherlow and Mountbrowne Shaun, which is no mean feat considering that these three dogs were from two different breeds and widely different characters and types. Harry was in charge of the training of the police dogs at Surrey under Sir Joseph Simpson's authority, and during those years in which he successfully handled dogs, he was also responsible for the breeding programme at the kennels which produced no less than eleven Working Trial Certificate winners under the Surrey Constabulary's prefix of Mountbrowne, most of which became champions. He was also responsible for training the handlers who worked these dogs, and it is a unique record unlikely to be repeated. His influence on police dogs and civilian Working Trials is still with us today. Between 1949 and 1968 the Surrey police dog section won no less than thirty-five Working Trial Certificates with fifteen of their dogs sharing these awards. Even though the Surrey police have not competed since

1968 it is a record that still stands and will take other police dog sections in this country many years to beat.

On the subject of records, only one handler has made four different dogs Working Trial Champions and that is the late and legendary Daphne Foreman. Daphne bred, trained and handled Alsatians under the kennel prefix of 'Hankley' and was a force to be reckoned with during her competitive days. Mrs A. C. Mason from the West Country established quite a record with her black Labradors. She was affectionately known as 'Min' to her friends, and amongst other things, those of us who witnessed some of the superb searches her dogs did in under two minutes, will not forget how she would be quite upset, in a nice sort of way, if her dogs took too long to bring all four articles out of the search. Her wonderful bitch, WT Champion Linnifold Blarney, made her mark by winning seven Tracking Dog Stake WT Certificates, and this is still the highest number of TD tickets won by one dog. Mrs Mason is probably the only handler to have won two Working Trial Certificates losing only half a mark. This she did with her Labrador bitch WTCh. Karadoc Zanella.

Until recently, Mr Peter Meanwell's Collie, WTCh. Petricas Laddie held the record number of tickets won by any dog. Laddie having won a total of six in the PD Stakes and three in the TD Stakes. However, the new record established by Mr Ted Buckle's Alsatian, WTCh. Tanfield Wystan, is a total of ten tickets, made up of seven in the PD Stakes and three in the TD Stakes.

During the late sixties the Kennel Club decided to make it compulsory for each society to hold an open Trial for each championship Trial held. The reason for this move was to help reduce the entries at championship events and to provide a vehicle for new judges to gain experience. Up until then a dog could start its competitive life in the Utility Dog Stake, and having qualified 'excellent' proceed into the Open Stake. This new ruling meant much more work for the handler and dog as by now the Working Dog Stake had been officially added to the schedule. A dog was now required to gain the equivalent marks for a qualification at The Open Trials in both UD and WD Stakes, as well as qualifying in the same stakes at Championship Trials. During the early seventies, sufficient marks in each group in the TD Stake at open Trials became compulsory prior to the dog being entered into this stake at championship Trials.

Once these open Trials had become a compulsory progression, without taking any account of the usual inflation, the cost to a handler of getting his dog to the top became at least doubled. Under these circumstances the Portsmouth Dog Training Club decided to run what became known as one-day Trials. Whilst the Trial was held over several days, the handler and dog completed their work all on the same day. Previously to do this, it had been usual for the dog and handler to complete the nosework on either the Thursday or Friday and return for the control and agility on the Saturday. This new system meant that for many handlers it would be unnecessary to stop away overnight. Today we have a system whereby approximately half of the Trials are organized on the old conventional system, with the balance being one-day events. The argument against the one-day Trial is that a lot of the 'last day' atmosphere is lost. With the conventional system a social life was developed, with most of the handlers meeting at the local hostelry on the nights that it was necessary to stay at the Trials. Many people feel that this social life and atmosphere must be retained at all costs for this camaraderie is a great part of the Trials scene.

Up until 1974 it was a reasonably simple matter to get a new judge approved to judge at a championship Trial. It then became necessary to introduce rules for judging qualifications to ensure that only those people who had the necessary experience could become leading judges.

Whilst the Working Trial Regulations drawn up in 1961 by the Sir Joseph Simpson sub-committee had been an excellent revision, the Kennel Club decided to allow the WT Council to propose a further revision, and after the council had set up their own sub-committee which reported back, the Kennel Club committee accepted the new regulations which came into effect from 1 January 1977 – the two main differences to the new schedule being the re-allocation of marks for the patrol group of the Police Dog Stake, and the alteration to the Companion Dog Stake elementary search exercise. This latter exercise has now been brought more into line with the search exercise in the other stakes, as it had been felt that the preceding regulations for this test had allowed many dogs to carry out a lucky retrieve rather than a search.

A big milestone along the path of Working Trial progress was reached in October 1975 when the first Kennel Club Working

Trial Championships were held at Enfield, Middlesex. Field Trials, Breed and Obedience Shows had for many years held an annual supreme event under Kennel Club auspices, and, following four years of discussions, the WT Championships eventually got under way. Each year the Kennel Club delegate the responsibility of staging this event to one of the Championship Working Trial Societies. It was fitting, in view of the tremendous part played by the ASPADS in the early years of the sport, that the honour of organizing the first event was given to them.

1976 saw the championships going to Lauder, Scotland, with the Scottish Working Trials Society organizing, and in 1977 the SATS staged the event in Sussex. Any dog that has won a Working Trial Certificate in a preceding twelve-month period is invited to take part in the championships. No handler has as yet declined to accept the honour of this invitation, and the event, already highly regarded by the handlers, is likely to grow in stature during the next few years. Both the Tracking Dog and the Police Dog Stakes are held, and it is the only event at which two Working Trial Certificates are awarded, one for each stake. The winners of this event so far are:

Tracking Dog Stake

1975 Mrs S. Hodson with WTCh. Linnifold Black Magic, Labrador Retriever.

1976 Mrs S. Hodson with WTCh. Linnifold Black Magic, Labrador Retriever.

Police Dog Stake

1975 PC Keith Lake for the Metropolitan Police with WTCh. Bois of Limbrook, Alsatian.

1976 Mr Peter Meanwell with Jamie of Petricas, Working Sheepdog (this, being the dog's second win, made him a WTCh.).

It can be seen that another record has been established by Mrs Susan Hodson winning the Tracking Dog Event for two years running with the same dog, which is no mean feat when one considers that, in both years, she was up against the best the country had to offer. No doubt the reader will have noticed that her dog bears the famous 'Linnifold' prefix of Mrs A. C. Mason, which indicates the better chance of success a handler has by purchasing from good working stock. No matter how good the dog's background, they still require training, and Susan does not appear to have made many mistakes.

Working Trials will undoubtedly grow in popularity as most sports will. For as time progresses, people find more and more leisure time on their hands and what better way to spend it than by training to a high standard and then competing with a dog? That high standard is the very reason why the handler and dog are a team. The mutual love and respect between a pet dog and his master is increased a thousand-fold once they have become that team.

It is to be hoped that Working Trials will always remain serious but yet light-hearted events, and that the social life they have enjoyed for many years continues.

APPENDIX A

Kennel Club Working Trial Regulations

1st January 1977

1. *Management of Working Trials.* – The management of a Working Trial shall be entrusted to a Working Trial Manager who shall be responsible for ensuring that the regulations are observed but he may not interfere with the Judges' decisions which shall be final.

The Working Trial Manager shall be appointed by the Committee of the Society holding the Trial who shall decide upon any matter not related to judging and not provided for in the Kennel Club Rules and Regulations for Working Trials and Obedience Classes and may call upon the Judge or Judges to assist with the decision which shall be final. The Working Trial Manager may not compete at the Trial and should be present throughout.

2. *Judges.* – When a Judge, from ill-health or any other unexpected cause, is prevented from attending or finishing a meeting, the Working Trial Manager once the Trial has commenced shall have the power of deciding what action is to be taken.

3. *Schedule.* – A Society holding a Working Trial must issue a schedule which is to be treated as a contract between the Society and the public and neither party is permitted to make any modification before the date of the Trial, except by permission of the Kennel Club, such alterations to be advertised in suitable publications where possible.

The schedule must contain:

(*a*) The date and place of the Working Trial.
(*b*) The latest date for applying for entry at the Trial. A separate official entry form which must be an exact copy of the wording of the specimen entry form issued by the Kennel Club.
(*c*) The amounts of entry fees and any prize money.
(*d*) The conditions of the draw for the order of running.

(*e*) The conditions and qualifications for making entries and for intimating acceptance or refusal of entries

(*f*) An announcement that the Working Trial is held under Kennel Club Working Trial Rules and Regulations with such exceptions and conditions as the committee of the Society may decide. Such exceptions and conditions must have received the approval of the General Committee of the Kennel Club prior to publication of the schedule.

(*g*) The definition of each Stake, together with the qualification or limitations for entry in that Stake.

(*h*) The names of Judges. An announcement that if the entries in the Companion Dog Stake exceed 30, a Judge may be appointed to judge the Elementary Search and the competitors notified accordingly.

4. *Assessing Weather Conditions.* – The Working Trial Manager and the Judges should assess the weather conditions and should they consider the weather unfit for holding the Trials the commencement may be postponed until such time as is considered necessary for the Trials to be abandoned and the entry fees returned.

5. *Handling of Dogs by Owner or his Deputy.* – An owner or handler may handle the dog, but it must be one or the other; and once the dogs have commenced work an owner must not interfere with his dog if he has deputed another person to handle it.

6. *Certification by Judge(s).* – The Judge(s) shall certify on a form provided by the Kennel Club that in their opinion the Stake was held in accordance with the Schedule and Kennel Club Rules and Regulations.

7. *Disqualification of Dogs.* – A dog shall be disqualified by the Judges and removed from the ground if in their opinion it is:

(*a*) Unfit to compete by reason of sexual causes.

(*b*) Suffering from any infectious or contagious disease.

(*c*) Interfering with the safety or chance of winning of an opponent.

(*d*) Of such temperament or is so much out of hand as to be a danger to the safety of any person or other animal.

(*e*) Likely to cause cruelty to the dog if it continues in the Trial.

If a dog competes which has been exposed to the risk of any contagious or infectious disease during the period of six weeks prior to the Working Trial and/or if any dog shall be proved to be suffering at a Working Trial from any contagious or infectious disease, the owner thereof shall be liable to be dealt with under Rule 9 of the Kennel Club Rules for Working Trials and Obedience Classes.

8. *Certificates.* – The Judge or Judges shall give certificates at a Championship Working Trial PD (Police Dog), TD (Tracking Dog), WD (Working Dog), UD (Utility Dog), and CD (Companion Dog) Stake to those dogs which have obtained 70% or more marks in each group of exercises in the Stake entered (provided that the dog has complied with any additional requirements for that Stake). The added qualification "Excellent" shall be awarded should the dog also obtain 80% or more marks of the total for the Stake.

Societies may issue these Qualification Certificates in Championship Stakes to their own design, subject to the approval of the Kennel Club but they must contain the name and breed of the dog, the name of the owner, the title of the Society and date of the Trials, the qualification and marks awarded and the signatures of the Judge and Working Trial Manager.

The Judge or Judges at Open Working Trials run to these schedules shall give Certificates of Merit for those dogs whose marks would have gained them a qualification 'Excellent' at a Championship Working Trial, provided that the Certificate contains the following words: 'This Certificate does not entitle the dog named thereon to any qualification recognized by the Kennel Club except entry in appropriate Stakes at Championship Working Trials'. Such Certificates of Merit must contain the name and breed of the dog, the name of the owner, the title of the Society and date of the Trial, the Stake and the marks awarded (without reference to any qualification) and the signatures of the Judge(s) and Working Trial Manager.

9. *Prizes.* –The winner of the Stake shall be the dog that has qualified with 70% or more marks in each group of the Stake and has obtained most marks. No dog that has not so qualified shall be placed in the prize list above a qualified dog. If no dog has qualified the dog with the highest number of marks may be awarded the prize. Judges are also empowered and instructed to withhold any prize or prizes if in their opinion the dogs competing do not show sufficient merit. Nothing in this Regulation shall apply to the award of 'Special' prizes.

10. *Penalties for impugning the decisions of the Judges.* – If anyone taking part in the Trials openly impugns the decision of the Judge or Judges, he is liable to be dealt with by the Committee under Rules 9 or 10 of the Kennel Club Rules for Working Trials and Obedience Classes.

11. *Order of Running.* – The order of running tracks shall be determined by a draw and competitors notified accordingly prior to the day of the Trial.

12. *Disqualification for Absence.* – The Working Trial Manager shall announce the specific time at which a dog or group of dogs may be called for any exercise or group of exercises. Each dog must be brought up at its proper time and in its proper turn without delay. If occasion demands the times and order may be changed at the discretion of the Working Trial Manager with the approval of the Judge or Judges, provided that no hardship is thereby caused to any competitor. If absent when called, the dog shall be liable to be disqualified by the Judge or Judges.

13. *Method of Working.* – The Judge or Judges in consultation with the Working Trial Manager may arrange for dogs to be working singly or together in any numbers. All dogs entered in a Stake shall be tested as far as possible under similar conditions.

14. *Regulations Regarding Handling.*

(*a*) A person handling a dog may speak, whistle or work it by hand signals as he wishes, but he can be called to order by the Judge or Judges for making unnecessary noise, and if he persists in doing so the Judge or Judges can disqualify the dog.

(*b*) No person shall carry out punitive correction or harsh handling of a dog.

15. *Awards.* – All awards made by the Judge or Judges at a Working Trial shall be in accordance with the agreed scale of points approved by the General Committee of the Kennel Club. Equal awards for any of the prizes offered at a Working Trial are prohibited.

16. *Notification of Awards.* – The Secretary of a Working Trial shall send (within 7 days of the Trial) the Judges' certification and two marked catalogues to the Kennel Club indicating the prize winners and those dogs to which the Judges have awarded Certificates.

17. *Entry Forms.* – Entry Forms must be in accordance with the approved form which must be issued by the Secretary of the Working Trial, and all entries must be made thereon and not otherwise, and entirely in ink; only one person shall enter on one form. All such entry

forms must be preserved by the Committee of a Working Trial meeting for at least twelve months from the last day of the Trial.

18. *Refusal of Entries.* – The Committee of any Meeting may reserve to themselves the right of refusing any entries on reasonable grounds.

19. *Objection to Dogs.* – An objection to a dog must be made to the Secretary in writing at any time within twenty-one days of the last day of the meeting upon the objector lodging with the Secretary the sum of £5.00. The deposit may be returned after the General Committee of the Kennel Club has considered the objection. Should any objection be made other than under Regulation 7(a) to 7(e) the dog should be allowed to compete and a full report made to the Kennel Club.

When an objection is lodged the Secretary of the Society must send to the Kennel Club:

(*a*) A copy of the objection.
(*b*) The name and address of the objector.
(*c*) The name and address of the owner of the dog.
(*d*) All relevant evidence.

The objection will then be dealt with by the General Committee of the Kennel Club whose decision shall be final.

No objection shall be invalidated solely on the grounds that it was incorrectly lodged.

If the dog objected to be disqualified, the prize to which it would otherwise have been entitled shall be forfeited, and the dog or dogs next in order of merit shall move up and take the prize or prizes.

No spectator, not being the owner of a dog competing, or his accredited representative has the right to lodge any objection to a dog or to any action taken at the meeting unless he be a member of the Committee of the Society or of the General Committee of the Kennel Club or a Steward. Any objection so lodged will be disregarded.

20. *Withdrawal of dogs from Competition.* – No dog entered for competition and actually at the meeting, may be withdrawn from competition without notice to the Working Trials Manager. No dog shall compulsorily be withdrawn from a Stake by reason of the fact that it has obtained less than 70% of the marks in any one group.

21. *Failure to Participate in Any Exercise.* – Failure to participate in any exercise in a group in any Stake shall result in failure to qualify in that group.

22. The Working Trials and Obedience Committee shall issue an Appendix to the Schedule of Exercises and Points, 'Description of

Exercises and Guidance for Judges and Competitors at Working Trials', which they may from time to time alter and in respect of which notice shall be given in the Kennel Gazette.

23. Working Trials for Bloodhounds shall be exempt from Working Trial Regulations 8, 9, 14(a), 15 and 21 and the Definitions of Stakes and Schedule of Exercises and Points. Until further notice the schedule of each Bloodhound Working Trial shall be submitted to the Kennel Club for approval before publication, in accordance with the provision of Rule 3 of the Kennel Club Rules for Working Trials and Obedience Classes.

DEFINITIONS OF STAKES

When entering for Championship or Open Working Trials, wins at Members Working Trials will not count.

No dog entered in PD or TD Stakes shall be eligible to enter in any other Stake at the meeting.

All Police dogs shall be considered qualified for entry in WD Championship Stakes if they hold the Regional Police Dog qualification 'Excellent', provided that such entries are countersigned by the Senior Police Officer I/C when such entries are made. Dogs holding this qualification are not eligible for entry in CD or UD Open or Championship Stakes, nor in WD Open Stakes.

No Working Trial Stake shall be limited to less that 30 dogs. If a limit is imposed on entries in any Stake, it shall be carried out by ballot after the date of closing of entries. Championship TD or PD Stakes shall not be limited by numbers in any way.

OPEN WORKING TRIAL

Companion Dog (CD) Stake. – For dogs which have not qualified CD Ex or UD Ex or won three or more first prizes in CD or any prize in UD Stakes, WD Stakes, PD or TD Stakes at Open or Championship Working Trials.

Utility Dog (UD) Stake. – For dogs which have not been awarded a Certificate of Merit in UD, WD, PD or TD Stakes.

Working Dog (WD) Stake. – For dogs which have been awarded a Certificate of Merit in UD Stakes but not in WD, PD or TD Stakes.

Tracking Dog (TD) Stake. – For dogs which have been awarded a Certificate of Merit in WD Stakes but not in TD Stakes.

Police Dog (PD) Stake. – For dogs which have been awarded a Certificate of Merit in WD Stakes.

CHAMPIONSHIP WORKING TRIAL

Companion Dog (CD) Stake. – For dogs which have not won three or more first prizes in CD Stakes or any prize in any other Stake at Championship Working Trials.

Utility Dog (UD) Stake. – For dogs which have won a Certificate of Merit in an Open UD Stake. A dog is not eligible for entry in this Stake if it has been entered in the WD Stake on the same day.

Working Dog (WD) Stake. – For dogs which have qualified UD Ex and have won a Certificate of Merit in Open WD Stakes.

Tracking Dog (TD) Stake. – For dogs which have qualified WD Ex and have won a Certificate of Merit in Open TD Stakes.

Police Dog (PD) Stake. – For dogs which have qualified WD Ex.

MEMBERS WORKING TRIAL

This is restricted to the members of the Society holding the Working Trial and eligibility for Stakes is as for Open Working Trials.

JUDGES AT CHAMPIONSHIP WORKING TRIALS

For CD Stake: Must have judged at least two Open Working Trials and have as a handler qualified a dog 'Excellent' in a Championship CD Stake.

For UD Stake: Must have judged UD or WD Stakes at two Open Trials, have judged CD Stakes at a Championship Trial and have as a handler qualified a dog 'Excellent' in a Championship WD Stake.

For WD Stake: Must have judged UD or WD Stakes at two Open Trials, UD Stake at a Championship Trial and have as a handler qualified a dog 'Excellent' in a Championship WD Stake.

For PD Stake and TD Stake: Must have judged at two Open Trials, WD Stake at a Championship Trial and qualified a dog 'Excellent' in the Stake for which he was nominated to judge.

Note: Service and Police judges are eligible to judge UD Stake at a Championship Trial provided they have qualified a dog WD 'Excellent'. They must qualify for approval for other Stakes as above, except that those who have judged all parts at Regional or National Police Dog Trials will not have to qualify as a civilian handler.

KENNEL CLUB WORKING TRIAL CHAMPIONSHIPS

(*a*) The Kennel Club Working Trial Championships at which Police Dog (PD) and Tracking Dog (TD) Stakes shall be scheduled are held annually.

(*b*) The responsibility for organizing the Championships each year will normally be delegated to a Working Trial Society approved to hold Championship Working Trials, such Society to be selected by the Working Trials and Obedience Committee from applications submitted by Societies. No Society to stage the event two years in succession.

(*c*) The Secretary of the Kennel Club will unless otherwise specified be the Working Trial Secretary for the event, the Society scheduling the Championships appointing a Trials Manager.

(*d*) The following shall be the method of selection of judges for the Championships: Nominated by Working Trials Societies which have been granted Championship Working Trial status for balloting by Working Trial Council, final selection by the Working Trials and Obedience Committee.

(*e*) Dogs eligible for entry in the Championships qualify as follows:

(*i*) *TD Championship:* A dog must have been placed 1st in Championship TD Stake and qualified 'Excellent' in the Stake during the period 1st October–30th September preceding the Championships.

(*ii*) *PD Championship:* A dog must have been placed 1st in Championship PD Stake and qualified 'Excellent' in the Stake during the period 1st October–30th September in the two years preceding the Championships.

(*iii*) Dogs which qualify as above in both PD and TD Championship Stakes are permitted to be entered in either or both Championship Stakes.

(*iv*) The Winners of the previous year's Championship Stakes qualify automatically.

(*v*) No other dogs are eligible for entry in the Championships except by special permission of the General Committee of the Kennel Club.

(*f*) The Championships will normally be held during the third weekend in October each year.

(*g*) The winner of each Stake in the Championships is entitled to the description of Working Trial Champion.

(*h*) The Working Trial Society selected to hold the Championships is allowed to forgo one Open Working Trial during the same year.

SCHEDULE OF EXERCISES AND POINTS
COMPANION DOG (CD) STAKE

	Marks	Group Total	Minimum Group Qualifying Mark
Group I. Control			
1. Heel on Leash	5		
2. Heel Free	10		
3. Recall to Handler	5		
4. Sending the dog away	10	30	21
Group II. Stays			
5. Sit (2 Minutes)	10		
6. Down (10 Minutes)	10	20	14
Group III. Agility			
7. Scale (3) Stay (2) Recall (5)	10		
8. Clear Jump	5		
9. Long Jump	5	20	14
Group IV. Retrieving and Nose			
10. Retrieve a dumb-bell	10		
11. Elementary Search	20	30	21
Totals	100	100	70

UTILITY DOG (UD) STAKE

	Marks	Group Total	Minimum Group Qualifying Mark
Group I. Control			
1. Heel Free	5		
2. Sending the dog away	10		
3. Retrieve a dumb-bell	5		
4. Down (10 minutes)	10		
5. Steadiness to gunshot	5	35	25
Group II. Agility			
6. Scale (3) Stay (2) Recall (5)	10		
7. Clear Jump	5		
8. Long Jump	5	20	14
Group III. Nosework			
9. Search	35		
10. Track (95) Article (15)	110	145	102
Totals	200	200	141

WORKING DOG (WD) STAKE

	Marks	Group Total	Minimum Group Qualifying Mark
Group I. Control			
1. Heel Free	5		
2. Sending the dog away	10		
3. Retrieve a dumb-bell	5		
4. Down (10 minutes)	10		
5. Steadiness to gunshot	5	35	25
Group II. Agility			
6. Scale (3) Stay (2) Recall (5)	10		
7. Clear Jump	5		
8. Long Jump	5	20	14
Group III. Nosework			
9. Search	35		
10. Track (90) Articles (10+10=20)	110	145	102
Totals	200	200	141

TRACKING DOG (TD) STAKE

	Marks	Group Total	Minimum Group Qualifying Mark
Group I. Control			
1. Heel Free	5		
2. Sendaway and Directional Control	10		
3. Speak on Command	5		
4. Down (10 minutes)	10		
5. Steadiness to gunshot	5	35	25
Group II. Agility			
6. Scale (3) Stay (2) Recall (5)	10		
7. Clear Jump	5		
8. Long Jump	5	20	14
Group III. Nosework			
9. Search	35		
10. Track (100) Articles (10+10+10=30)	130	165	116
Totals	220	220	155

POLICE DOG (PD) STAKE

	Marks	Group Total	Minimum Group Qualifying Mark
Group I. Contro			
1. Heel Free	5		
2. Sendaway and Directional Control	10		
3. Speak on Command	5		
4. Down (10 minutes)	10		
5. Steadiness to gunshot	5	35	25
Group II. Agility			
6. Scale (3) Stay (2) Recall (5)	10		
7. Clear Jump	5		
8. Long Jump	5	20	14
Group III. Nosework			
9. Search	35		
10. Track (60) Articles (10+10=20)	80	115	80
Group IV. Patrol			
11. Quartering the Ground	45		
12. Test of Courage	20		
13. Search and Escort	25		
14a. Recall from Criminal	30		
14b. Pursuit and Detention of Criminal	30	150	105
Totals	320	320	224

DESCRIPTION OF EXERCISES AND GUIDANCE FOR JUDGES AND COMPETITORS AT WORKING TRIALS

A. *Method of Handling.* – Although implicit obedience to all orders is necessary, dogs and handlers must operate in as free and natural a manner as possible. Excessive formalism may be penalized, particularly if, in the opinion of the Judge, it detracts from the ability of the dog to exercise its senses in relation to all that is happening in the vicinity. Persistent barking, whining etc. in any exercise other than location of articles, person or speak on command should be penalized. Food may not be given to the dog by the handler whilst being tested.

B. *Heel Work.* – The Judge should test the ability of the dog to keep his shoulder reasonably close to the left knee of the handler who should walk smartly in his natural manner at normal, fast and slow paces through turns and among and around persons and obstacles. The halt, with the dog sitting to heel and a 'figure of eight' may be included at any stage.

Any act, signal or command or jerking of the leash which in the opinion of the Judge has given the dog unfair assistance shall be penalized.

C. *Sit (2 Minutes).* – Dogs may be tested individually or in a group or groups. The Judge or Steward will give the command 'last command' and handlers should then instantly give their final commands to the dogs. Any further commands or signals to the dogs will be penalized. Handlers will then be instructed to leave their dogs and proceed to positions indicated by the Judge or Steward until ordered to return to them. Where possible, such positions should be out of sight of the dogs but bearing in mind the short duration of the exercise this may not be practical. Dogs must remain in the sit position throughout the test until the Judge or Steward indicates that the test has finished. Minor movements must be penalized. The Judge may use his discretion should interference by another dog cause the dog to move.

D. *Down (10 Minutes).* – Handlers must be out of sight of the dogs who may be tested individually or in a group or groups. The Judge or Steward will give the command 'last command' and handlers should then instantly give their final commands to their dogs. Any further commands or signals to the dogs will be penalized. Handlers will then be instructed to leave their dogs and proceed to positions indicated by the Judge or Steward until ordered to return to them. Dogs must remain in the 'Down' position throughout the test until the Judge or Steward indicates that the Test has finished. No dog will be awarded any marks that sits, stands or crawls more than its approximate body length in any direction. Minor movements must be penalized. The Judge may use his discretion should interference by another dog cause a dog to move. The Judge may test the dogs by using distractions but may not call it by name.

E. *Recall to Handler.* – The dog should be recalled from the 'Down' or 'sit' position. The handler being a reasonable distance from the dog at the discretion of the Judge. The dog should return at a smart pace and sit in front of the handler, afterwards going smartly to heel on command or signal. Handler to await command of the Judge or Steward.

F. *Retrieve a Dumb-bell.* – The dog should not move forward to retrieve nor deliver to hand on return until ordered by the handler on the Judge or Stewards' instructions. The Retrieve should be executed at a smart pace without mouthing or playing with the object. After delivery the handler will send his dog to heel on the instructions of the Judge or Steward.

G. *Send Away and Directional Control.* – The minimum distance that the Judge shall set for the Send Away shall be 20 yards for the CD Stake and 50 yards for all other Stakes. The TD and PD Stakes shall also include a redirection of a minimum of 50 yards. When the dog has reached the designated point or the Judge is satisfied that after a reasonable time the handler cannot improve the position of the dog by any further commands the dog should be stopped in either the stand, sit or down position at the discretion of the handler. At this point in the TD or PD Stakes the Judge or Steward shall instruct the handler to redirect his dog. In all Stakes, whilst the Judge should take into account the number of commands used during the exercise, importance should be placed upon the handler's ability to direct his dog to the place indicated.

H. *Steadiness to Gunshot.* – The most appropriate occasion of testing this exercise would be in open country. The dog may be either walking at heel free or be away from the handler who must be permitted to remain within controlling distance whilst the gun is fired. Any sign of fear, aggressiveness or barking must be penalized. This test shall not be carried out without prior warning, or incorporated in any other test. The Judge will not provoke excitement by excessive display of the gun, nor shall the gun be pointed at the dog.

I. *Speak on Command.* – The Judge will control the position of the handler in relation to the dog and may require the handler to work the dog walking at heel. If the dog is not required to walk at heel, the handler may at his discretion place the dog in the stand, sit or down. The dog will be ordered to speak and cease speaking on command of the Judge or Steward who may then instruct the handler to make the dog speak again. Speaking should be sustained by the dog whilst required with the minimum of commands and/or signals. Continuous and/or excessive incitements to speak shall be severely penalized. This test should not be incorporated with any other test.

J. *Agility.* – No part of the scale or clear or long jump equipment to be traversed by a dog shall be less than three feet wide nor be in any way injurious to the dog. The tests shall be followed in a sequence agreed by the Judge and will commence with the Scale. The Scale should be a vertical wall of wooden planks and may have affixed on both sides three slats evenly distributed in the top half of the jump. The top surface of the Scale may be lightly padded. The handler should approach the Scale at a walking pace and halt four to nine feet in front of it and in his own time order the dog to scale. On reaching the other side the dog should be ordered to stay in the stand, sit or down position, the handler having previously nominated such a position to the Judge The Judge should ensure that the dog will stay steady and may indicate to the handler where he should stand in relation to his dog and the Scale before ordering the dog to be recalled over the Scale. A dog which fails to go over the Scale at the second attempt shall be excluded from the stay and recall over the Scale. Failure in the recall over the Scale does not disqualify from marks previously gained.

The handler may either approach the clear and long jumps with the dog or send it forward or stand by the jumps and call the dog up to jump. At no time should the handler proceed beyond any part of the jumps before they have been traversed by the dog. Once the dog has cleared the obstacle he should remain on the other side under control until joined by the handler. The clear jump should be so constructed that it will be obvious if the dog has exerted more than slight pressure upon it. The rigid top bar may be fixed or rest in cups and the space below may be filled in but the filling should not project above the bottom of the top bar. Appreciable pressure exerted by the dog on the clear jump shall be considered to be a failure. Casual fouling with fore or hind legs will be penalized at the discretion of the Judge. Failure or refusal at any of the three types of jump may be followed by a second attempt and any one such failure shall be penalized by at least 50% of the marks allotted to that part of the exercise in which the dog is given a second attempt.

Jumping heights and lengths:

COMPANION DOG (CD) STAKE AND UTILITY DOG (UD) STAKE

(*a*) *Scale*

Dogs not exceeding 10 in. at shoulder	3 ft
Dogs not exceeding 15 in. at shoulder	4 ft
Dogs exceeding 15 in. at shoulder	6 ft

(*b*) *Clear Jump*

Dogs not exceeding 10 in. at shoulder	1 ft 6 in.
Dogs not exceeding 15 in. at shoulder	2 ft
Dogs exceeding 15 in. at shoulder	3 ft

(*c*) *Long Jump*

Dogs not exceeding 10 in. at shoulder	4 ft
Dogs not exceeding 15 in. at shoulder	6 ft
Dogs exceeding 15 in. at shoulder	9 ft

WORKING DOG (WD) STAKE TRACKING DOG (TD) STAKE AND POLICE DOG (PD) STAKE

(*a*) Scale	6 ft
(*b*) Clear Jump	3 ft
(*c*) Long Jump	9 ft

K. *Search.* – The Companion Dog (CD) Stake Search shall contain three articles and all other Stakes shall contain four articles. In all Stakes fresh articles must be placed for each dog who must recover a minimum of two articles to qualify. As a guide the articles should be similar in size to a six-inch nail or a match box, but the Judge should choose articles in relation to the nature of the ground and the Stake which he is judging. The time allotted shall be four minutes in the CD Stake and five minutes in all other Stakes. The articles should be well handled and placed by a Steward who shall foil the ground by walking in varying directions over the area. Each competitor shall have a separate piece of land.

The CD Stake search area shall be 15 yards square, all other Stakes being 25 yards square and shall be clearly defined by a marker peg at each corner. The handler may work his dog from any position outside the area, provided that he does not enter it.

In the CD Stake a maximum five marks should be allotted for each article and a maximum five marks for style and control. In all other Stakes a maximum seven marks should be allotted for each article and a maximum seven marks for style and control.

L. *Track.* – The track should be plotted on the ground to be used for the nosework by Stewards previous to the day of commencement of the Trials. An area of ground which has had a track laid over it must not have another track laid over it until the following day. The track shall be single line and may include turns. The articles should be in keeping with the nature of the ground. There shall be a marker left by the track layer to indicate the start of the track. In the UD Stake a second marker should be left not more than 30 yards from the start to indicate the direction of the first leg.

Unless the Judge considers the dog to have lost the track beyond recovery or has run out of the time allotted for the completion of the track a handler may recast his dog at his discretion. The Judge should not at any time indicate to the handler where he should recast his dog except in exceptional circumstances.

The track shall be approximately half a mile long and should be laid as far as possible by a stranger to the dog. The article(s) should be well scented. When the judging is in progress the track-layer shall be present at the side of the Judge to indicate the exact line of the track and the position of the articles.

The UD Stake track shall be not less than half an hour old and shall include one article at the end, recovery of the article not being a requirement for qualification.

The WD and PD Stake tracks shall be not less than one and a half hours old and shall include two articles one of which must be recovered to qualify.

The TD Stake track shall be not less than three hours old and shall include three articles two of which must be recovered to qualify.

In all Stakes the last article shall indicate the end of the track. No two articles should be laid together.

A spare track additional to requirements should be laid but the opportunity to run a new track should be given only in exceptional circumstances.

The area used for Tracking is out of bounds to all competitors for practice Tracks and exercise from the time of the first track and any competitor found contravening this instruction is liable to be disqualified by the Judge and/or Stewards from participating in the Trial in accordance with the provision of Regulation No 7(c).

The dog must be worked on a harness and tracking line.

M. *Quartering the Ground.* – The missing person or criminal should be protected to the minimum extent consistent with safety. He should remain motionless out of sight of the handler, but should be accessible on investigation to a dog which has winded him.

The Judge should satisfy himself that the dog has found the person and has given warning spontaneously and emphatically without being directed by the handler. Once the person has been detected and the dog has given voice, he may offer meat or other food which should be refused by the dog. If the dog ignores the food he may throw it on the ground in front of the dog. A dog which bites the person or criminal must be severely penalized.

N. *Test of Courage.* – This is a test of courage rather than of control. Dogs will not be heavily penalized in this test for lack of control. Handlers must be prepared to have the dog tested when on the lead by an unprotected Judge or Steward, and/or when off the lead by a protected Steward. The method of testing will be at the discretion of the Judge.

O. *Search and Escort.* – The criminal will be searched by the handler with the dog off the lead at the sit, stand or down. The Judge will assess whether the dog is well placed tactically and ready to defend if called to do so.

The handler will then be told to escort the prisoner(s) at least 30 yards in a certain direction, he will give at least one turn on the direction of the Judge. During the exercise the criminal will turn and attempt to overcome the handler. The dog may defend spontaneously or on command and must release the criminal at once both when he stands still or when the handler calls him off. The handler should be questioned as to his tactics in positioning the dog in both search and escort.

P. *Recall from Criminal.* (Exercise 14(a)). – The criminal, protected to the minimum extent consistent with safety, will be introduced to the handler whose dog will be free at heel. After an unheated conversation the criminal will run away. At a reasonable distance the handler will be ordered to send his dog. When the dog is approximately halfway between handler and the criminal he will be ordered to be recalled. The recall may be by whistle or voice. The criminal should continue running until the dog returns or closes. If the dog continues to run alongside the criminal the criminal should run a further ten or dozen paces to indicate this.

Q. *Pursuit and Detention of Criminal.* (Exercise 14(b)). – The criminal (a different one for choice) and handler should be introduced as above, and the dog sent forward under the same conditions. The criminal must continue to attempt to escape and, if possible, should do so through some exit or in some vehicle once the dog has had a chance to catch up with him. The dog must be regarded as having succeeded if it clearly prevents the criminal from continuing his line of flight, either by holding him by the arm, knocking him over or close circling him till he becomes giddy. If the dog fails to make a convincing attempt to detain the criminal, it shall lose any marks that it may have obtained under exercise 14(a) or alternatively, it shall not be tested on exercise 14(a) if that follows exercise 14(b).

Appendix B

WINNERS OF WORKING TRIAL CERTIFICATES FROM 1927

Stake	*Dog*	*Sex*	*Breed*	*Handler*	*Owner*	*Judge*
Open	*1927* Crumstone Amigo	D	Alsatian	Mr W. F. Colbourne	Mr W. F. Colbourne	AVM C. L. Lambe Mr J. S. D. Harries-Jones Mr H. Robbins
Open	Asra Von Schurzfell	B	Alsatian	Miss J. Workman	Mms E. R. and J. Workman	Herr Hans Rothemund
Open	*1928* Aston Von Rathenau Schlucht	D	Alsatian	Miss J. Workman	Mms E. R. and J. Workman	Maj. C. E. W. Beddoes Mr J. S. D. Harries-Jones
Open	Asra Von Schurzfell	B	Alsatian	Miss J. Workman	Mms E. R. and J. Workman	Mr E. F. Ringwood
Open	Asra Von Schurzfell	B	Alsatian	Miss J. Workman	Mms E. R. and J. Workman	Herr L. Bodenstab
Open	Tective Nade	n.k.	Alsatian	Mr J. Radcliffes	Mr J. Radcliffes	AVM C. L. Lambe Mr L de Pinto
Open	Crumstone Amigo	D	Alsatian	Mr W. F. Colbourne	Mr W. F. Colbourne	Mr H. Robbins Mr W. Roh

Stake	*Dog*	*Sex*	*Breed*	*Handler*	*Owner*	*Judge*
	1929					
Open	Asra Von Schurzfell	B	Alsatian	Miss J. Workman	Mms E. R. and J. Workman	Mr C. E. Rattee
Open	Brutus Boy	D	Alsatian	Mr C. E. Rattee	Mr C. E. Rattee	Mr L. H. de Pinto
Open	Asra Von Schurzfell	B	Alsatian	Miss J. Workman	Mms E. R. and J. Workman	Dr K. Reseback Herr A. Blumenthal
	1930					
Open	Buff of Cheyney	D	Alsatian	Mrs R. M. Cardwell	Mrs R. M. Cardwell	Mr W. F. Colbourne
Open	Brutus Boy	D	Alsatian	Mr C. E. Rattee	Mr C. E. Rattee	Miss J. Workman
Open	Brutus Boy	D	Alsatian	Mr C. E. Rattee	Mr C. E. Rattee	Mr J. S. D. Harries-Jones
Open	Susi Von Boll	B	Alsatian	Miss J. Workman	Mms E. R. and J. Workman	Herr L. Bodenstab and Mr O. Sautter
	1931					
Open	Crumberg Ruby of Belvale	B	Alsatian	Miss B. Kelly	Miss B. Kelly	Capt. J. Radcliffe
Open	Brutus Boy	D	Alsatian	Mr C. E. Rattee	Mr C. E. Rattee	Mr L. H. de Pinto
Open	Buff of Cheyney	D	Alsatian	Mrs R. M. Cardwell	Mrs R. M. Cardwell	Mr J. S. D. Harries-Jones
Open	Peter of Ninham	D	Alsatian	Mrs F. Roberts	Mrs F. Roberts	Mr C. E. Rattee
	1932					
Open	Flora Tacoma of Rigi	B	Alsatian	Miss D. Homan	Miss D. Homan	Mr J. S. D. Harries-Jones

Open	Wendla of Send	B	Gt Dane	Mr G. Stewart	Mr G. Stewart	Mr L. H. de Pinto
Open	Dewet Von Rossenberg of Pinefold	D	Alsatian	Mrs M. Girdwood	Mrs M. Girdwood	Mrs R. M. Cardwell
Open	Buff of Cheyney	D	Alsatian	Mrs R. M. Cardwell	Mrs R. M. Cardwell	Mr G. Robertson
Open	Tansy of Send	B	Gt Dane	Mr G. Stewart	Mr G. Stweart	Lady K. Ritson
	1933					
Open	Flora Tacoma of Rigi	B	Alsatian	Miss D. Homan	Miss D. Homan	Mr P. L. C. Gurney
Open	Asra Von Schurzfell	B	Alsatian	Miss J. Workman	Mms E. R. and J. Workman	Mr P. L. C. Gurney
Open	Flora Tacoma of Rigi	B	Alsatian	Miss D. Homan	Miss D. Homan	Mr L. H. de Pinto
	1934					
Open	Flora Tacoma of Rigi	B	Alsatian	Miss D. Homan	Miss D. Homan	Mr P. L. C. Gurney
Open	Salturn Peter	D	Alsatian	Mrs G. Salter and Mr C. W. Turner	Mrs G. Salter and Mr C. W. Turner	Miss J. M. A. Workman
Open	Hunding of Ceara	n.k.	Alsatian	Mr Dinsdale	Mr Dinsdale	Mr P. L. C. Gurney
Open	Flora Tacoma of Rigi	B	Alsatian	Miss D. Homan	Miss D. Homan	Mr G. Sly
	1935					
Open	Salturn Peter	D	Alsatian	Mrs G. Salter and Mr C. W. Turner	Mrs G. Salter and Mr C. W. Turner	Mrs F. Donaldson
Open	Ch. Susette	B	Poodle	Miss J. Rochford	Miss J. Rochford	Mr P. L. C. Gurney
Open	Flora Tacoma of Rigi	B	Alsatian	Miss D. Homan	Miss D. Homan	Miss J. Workman

Stake	*Dog*	*Sex*	*Breed*	*Handler*	*Owner*	*Judge*
Open	*1936* Salturn Peter	D	Alsatian	Mrs G. Salter and Mr C. W. Turner	Mrs G. Salter and Mr C. W. Turner	Miss J. Workman
Open	Flora Tacoma of Rigi	B	Alsatian	Miss D. Homan	Miss D. Homan	Capt. L. H. de Pinto
Open	Coleen of Rigi	B	Alsatian	Mr O. W. Sugden	Mr O. W. Sugden	Mr P. L. C. Gurney
Open	*1937* Brutus Girl of Seale	B	Alsatian	Mrs M. Howard	Mrs M. Howard	Mr A. E. Farmer
Open	Ch. Benign of Picardy	D	Alsatian	Miss D. Homan	Miss D. Homan	Miss J. Workman
Open	Ch. Benign of Picardy	D	Alsatian	Miss D. Homan	Miss D. Homan	Mr P. L. C. Gurney
Open	Brutus Girl of Seale	B	Alsatian	Mrs M. Howard	Mrs M. Howard	Mr G. Sly
Open	*1938* Amigo Seehim	D	Alsatian	Mr H. P. Colbourne	Mr H. P. Colbourne	Mrs E. M. Farmer
Open	Coleen of Rigi	B	Alsatian	Miss D. Homan	Miss D. Homan	Mr G. Sly
Open	Coleen of Rigi	B	Alsatian	Miss D. Homan	Miss D. Homan	Mr P. L. C. Gurney
Open	Amigo Seehim	D	Alsatian	Mr H. P. Colbourne	Mr H. P. Colbourne	Mrs M. Howard
Open	*1939* Coleen of Rigi	B	Alsatian	Miss D. Homan	Miss D. Homan	Mr G. Sly
Open	Moonen Shiel	B	Sheltie	Miss M. E. Osborne	Miss M. E. Osborne	Miss J. Workman
Open	Amigo Seehim	D	Alsatian	Mr H. P. Colbourne	Mr H. P. Colbourne	Mrs M. Howard

Open	*1947* Silva of Rigi	B	Alsatian	Miss D. Homan	Miss D. Homan	Mr Cuthbertson
Open	*1948* Rockswall Bello Romana	D	Alsatian	Mr H. P. Colbourne	Mr H. P. Colbourne	Mr G. Sly
Open	Sigurd of Jotunheim	D	Alsatian	Mr G. K. Hudson	Mr G. K. Hudson	Mr P. L. C. Gurney
Open	*1949* Ulf Von Margarethenhof	D	D'mann	PS H. Darbyshire	CC of Surrey	Mrs G. Hester
Open	Frenchcourt Ripple	B	Labrador	Mr J. Simpson	Mr J. Simpson	Mr R. M. Montgomery
Open	Rockswall Bello Romana	D	Alsatian	Mr H. P. Colbourne	Mr H. P. Colbourne	Miss H. D. Homan
Open	*1950* Loki of Hatherlow	D	Alsatian	Mr H. Darbyshire	Mr H. Darbyshire	Mr K. Hudson
Open	Crumstone Alouette of Rigi	B	Alsatian	Miss D. Homan	Miss D. Homan	Capt. P. L. C. Gurney
Open	Ulf Von Margarethenhof	D	D'mann	PS H. Darbyshire	CC of Surrey	Miss D. Homan
Open	Frenchcourt Ripple	B	Labrador	Mr J. Simpson	Mr J. Simpson	Mrs G. M. Barrington
Open	*1951* Loki of Hatherlow	D	Alsatian	Mr H. Darbyshire	Mr H. Darbyshire	Mrs G. Hester
Open	Sigurd of Jotunheim	D	Alsatian	Mr G. K. Hudson	Mr G. K. Hudson	PS H. Darbyshire
Open	Loki of Hatherlow	D	Alsatian	Mr H. Darbyshire	Mr H. Darbyshire	Mr R. M. Montgomery
Open	Frenchcourt Ripple	B	Labrador	Mrs J. Simpson	Mrs J. Simpson	Mr K. Butler
Open	Loki of Hatherlow	D	Alsatian	Mr H. Darbyshire	Mr H. Darbyshire	Mr G. Sly

Stake	*Dog*	*Sex*	*Breed*	*Handler*	*Owner*	*Judge*
	1952					
Open	Kandy of Rockswall	B	Alsatian	Miss V. M. Rice	Miss V. M. Rice	Mrs J. Simpson
Open	Angus of Heronsmoor	D	Alsatian	Mrs R. M. Montgomery	Mrs R. M. Montgomery	Miss H. D. Homan
Open	Mountbrowne Jenny	B	D'mann	PS Jones	CC of Buckinghamshire	Capt. P. L. C. Gurney
Open	Loki of Hatherlow	D	Alsatian	Mr H. Darbyshire	Mr H. Darbyshire	Mrs G. Hester
	1953					
Open	Loki of Hatherlow	D	Alsatian	Mr H. Darbyshire	Mr H. Darbyshire	Capt. R. Sharp
Open	Mountbrowne Julie	B	D'mann	PS T. Sessford	CC of Durham	Mr A. E. Farmer
Open	Mountbrowne Joe	D	D'mann	Mrs M. Porterfield	Mrs M. Porterfield	PS H. Darbyshire
Open	Mountbrowne Julie	B	D'mann	PS T. Sessford	CC of Durham	Mrs Harrison
	1954					
Open	Wanda of Tankersley	B	Labrador	Miss U. Ogle	Miss U. Ogle	Mrs A. M. Hester
Open	Mountbrowne Largo	D	Alsatian	PS A. Osment	CC of Surrey	Mrs M. Porterfield
Open	Mountbrowne Lorna	B	Alsatian	PC Williams	CC of Lancashire	Mr G. Sly
Open	Mountbrowne Karen	B	D'mann	PC B. Ling	CC of Surrey	Mrs J. Simpson
	1955					
Open	Mountbrowne Largo	D	Alsatian	PS A. Osment	CC of Surrey	Lt Col J. Y. Baldwin
Open	Mountbrowne Largo	D	Alsatian	PS A. Osment	CC of Surrey	Mr R. Matchell

Open	Mountbrowne Karen	B	D'mann	PC B. Ling	CC of Surrey	Mrs M. Porterfield
Open	Mountbrowne Miska	B	Alsatian	PC F. Riley	CC of Surrey	Mr R. Darbyshire
Open	Mountbrowne Julie	B	D'mann	PS T. Sessford	CC of Durham	PS H. Darbyshire
Open	Mountbrowne Nero	D	Alsatian	PC L. Truss	CC of Surrey	Capt. R. Sharp
	1956					
Open	Mountbrowne Danny	D	Alsatian	PC A. Atkinson	CC of Surrey	Mrs M. Porterfield
Open	Joseph of Aycliffe	D	D'mann	Mr W. McGorrigan	CC of Durham	Mr R. Darbyshire
Open	Ob.Ch. Amaryllis of Helmdon	B	Alsatian	Mrs D. Foreman	Mrs D. Foreman	PS A. N. Osment
TD	Emma of Woffra	B	Alsatian	Miss J. Oldacre	Miss J. Oldacre	Mrs G. M. Barrington
PD	Mountbrowne Shaun	D	Alsatian	PS H. Darbyshire	CC of Surrey	Mrs G. M. Barrington
Open	Ob. Ch. Amaryllis of Helmdon	B	Alsatian	Mrs D. Foreman	Mrs D. Foreman	Mr R. Matchell
Open	Squib of Parlington	D	Alsatian	Mr K. Cheetham	CC of West Riding	Mr R. Ling
	1957					
TD	Mountbrowne Largo	D	Alsatian	PS A. Osment	CC of Surrey	Mr A. E. Farmer
PD	Mountbrowne Shaun	D	Alsatian	PS H. Darbyshire	CC of Surrey	Mr. R. Ling
TD	Foxhanger Gay	B	Labrador	Mrs J. Simpson	Mrs J. Simpson	Herr H. Hitschold
PD	Abbotsway Randy	D	Boxer	Mrs A. M. West	Mrs A. M. West	Mr J. R. Witts

Stake	*Dog*	*Sex*	*Breed*	*Handler*	*Owner*	*Judge*
Open	Mountbrowne Visor	D	Alsatian	Mr J. Todd	CC of Edinburgh	Mr H. Darbyshire
Open	Cito of Maco	D	Alsatian	Mr R. Matchell	Mr R. Matchell	Mrs B. Langley
Open	Mountbrowne Umbra	B	Alsatian	PC G. Hearnden	CC of Surrey	Mrs M. Porterfield
	1958					
TD	Mountbrowne Umbra	B	Alsatian	PC G. Hearnden	CC of Surrey	Mr H. Darbyshire
PD	Sannox Rory Dhu	D	Boxer	Mrs A. M. West	Mrs A. M. West	Mr R. Matchell
TD	Isabelle of Rozavel	B	Alsatian	Miss U. Ogle	Miss U. Ogle	Mr A. N. Osment
PD	Mountbrowne Shaun	D	Alsatian	PS H. Darbyshire	CC of Surrey	Mr R. Darbyshire
PD	Mountbrowne Shaun	D	Alsatian	PS H. Darbyshire	CC of Surrey	Mr W. Redwood
PD	Mountbrowne Shaun	D	Alsatian	PS H. Darbyshire	CC of Surrey	Mr R. Ling
TD	Ord of Brittas	D	Alsatian	PC F. Booker	CC of Surrey	Mrs G. M. Harrington
TD	Emma of Woffra	B	Alsatian	Miss J. Oldacre	Miss J. Oldacre	Mr R. M. Montgomery
PD	Anna of Aycliffe	B	D'mann	PC R. Hutchinson	CC of Durham	Mr C. Fricker
	1959					
TD	Mountbrowne Ullah	D	Alsatian	PC J. Horn	CC of Durham	Mr H. Darbyshire
PD	Quest of Pasha	D	Alsatian	Mr J. Comber	Mr J. Comber	Mr R. M. Montgomery
TD	Ob. Ch. Southdown Caspia	B	Alsatian	Mrs D. Foreman	Mrs D. Foreman	Mr J. A. Morphy

PD	Mountbrowne Vagus	D	Alsatian	PC G. Wraight	CC of Surrey	Mr H. Darbyshire
PD	Mountbrowne Ullah	D	Alsatian	PC J. Horn	CC of Durham	Mr T. Sessford
PD	Arno of Aycliffe	D	D'mann	PC T. Aikenhead	CC of Durham	Sir Joseph Simpson and Mrs A. Montgomery
TD	Ob. Ch. Southdown Caspia	B	Alsatian	Mrs D. Foreman	Mrs D. Foreman	Lady Simpson
TD	*1960* Ob. Ch. Amaryllis of Helmdon	B	Alsatian	Mrs D. Foreman	Mrs D. Foreman	Mrs R. M. Montgomery
TD	Mountbrowne Vagus	D	Alsatian	PC G. Wraight	CC of Surrey	Capt. P.L. C. Gurney
TD	Foxhanger Maize	B	Labrador	Miss D. N. Gowland	Miss D. N. Gowland	Mrs J. Faulks
PD	Joseph of Aycliffe	D	D'mann	Mr W. McGorrigan	CC of Durham	Mrs M. Porterfield
PD	Mountbrowne Kosta	D	Alsatian	PC L. Truss	CC of Surrey	Mr T. Kane
PD	Sannox Rory Dhu	D	Boxer	Mrs A. M. West	Mrs A. M. West	Mr H. Darbyshire
TD	Quest of Pasha	D	Alsatian	Mr J. Comber	Mr J. Comber	Mr R. Ling
TD	Bruin of Mallion	D	R'weiler	Mrs M. Wait	Mrs M. Wait	Mr A. N. Osment
PD	Mountbrowne Kyloe	D	Alsatian	PC D. Johnson	CC of Bristol	Mrs A. M. West and Mr R. Matchell
TD	*1961* Sandpits Superb	D	Alsatian	Mr H. Bennett	Mr H. Bennett	Mrs G. M. Barrington
TD	Montmusk Max	D	Alsatian	PC R. Tee	CC of Dorset	Sir Joseph Simpson

Stake	*Dog*	*Sex*	*Breed*	*Handler*	*Onwner*	*Judge*
PD	Kim of Bucksgrove	D	Alsatian	N.K.	CC of Buckingham-shire	Lady Simpson
TD	Ob. Ch. Amaryllis of Helmdon	B	Alsatian	Mrs D. Foreman	Mrs D. Foreman	Miss U. Ogle
PD	Dunelm Jamie	D	Alsatian	Mr D. Needham	CC of Lincolnshire	Insp. T. Sessford
PD	Hankley Andromeda	B	Alsatian	Mrs D. Foreman	Mrs D. Foreman	Mr R. Darbyshire
PD	Dunelm Jamie	D	Alsatian	Mr D. Needham	CC of Lincolnshire	Capt. P. L. C. Gurney
PD	Quest of Ardfern	D	Alsatian	Mr J. Cree	Mr J. Cree	Mr W. McGorrigan
TD	Silver Carlos	D	Alsatian	Mr W. Champion	CC of East Sussex	Mr K. Cheetham
PD	Dianton Taurus	D	Alsatian	Mr W. Chadwick	Mr W. Chadwick	Mr R. M. Montgomery and Mr A. N. Osment
TD	FT Ch. Foxhanger Maize	B	Labrador	Miss D. M. Gowland	Miss D. M. Gowland	Mrs D. Foreman
TD	*1962* Lancon Heidi	B	Alsatian	PC R. H. Williamson	CC of Essex	Miss U. M. Ogle
TD	Bruin of Mallion	D	R'weiler	Mrs M. Wait	Mrs M. Wait	Mr R. M. Montgomery
TD	Sergeant of Barnhill	D	Alsatian	Mr D. J. Mutter	Mr D. J. Mutter	Mrs M. Porterfield
PD	Metpol Peter	D	Alsatian	PC R. Beale	Commissioner of Police of the Metropolis	Mrs A. M. West

TD	Sussex Barker	D	Alsatian	PC J. Bostock	CC of East Sussex	Mr T. Shelton
PD	Quest of Ardfern	D	Alsatian	Mr J. Cree	Mr J. Cree	Mr T. Kane
PD	Rolph of Friarsdown	D	Alsatian	Mr K. Cheetham	Mr K. Cheetham	Mr H. Darbyshire
PD	Horbent Ajax	D	Alsatian	PC R. Hutchinson	CC of Durham	Mr K. Cheetham
PD	Cito of Maco	D	Alsatian	Mr R. Matchell	Mr R. Matchell	Insp. J. Blackhall
TD	Rolph of Friarsdown	D	Alsatian	Mr K. Cheetham	Mr K. Cheetham	Mr R. Ling
TD	Ballerina of Hankley	B	Alsatian	Mrs D. Foreman	Mrs D. Foreman	Mr R. Plumridge
PD	Metpol Thor	D	Alsatian	PS P. Burnell	Receiver of the Metropolitan Police	Mrs D. Foreman and Mr J. A. Morphy
	1963					
TD	Karadoc Zanella	B	Labrador	Mrs J. S. Mason	Mr and Mrs J. S. Mason	Mr L. A. Pearce
TD	Kurt of Bourne	D	Alsatian	PC P. Colfer	CC of Bournemouth	Miss U. Ogle
TD	Sannox Patsy	B	Alsatian	Mr A. J. West	Mr A. J. West	Capt. P. L. C. Gurney
PD	Dianton Taurus	D	Alsatian	Mr W. Chadwick	Mr W. Chadwick	Mr R. Plumridge
TD	Max of Buckingham	D	Alsatian	PC J. Weston	CC of Buckinghamshire	Mr A. N. Osment
PD	Dagenite Rebel	D	Alsatian	Mr A. Robinson	CC of Lincolnshire	Mr K. Cheetham
PD	Vikkas Saracen Av Hvitsand	D	Alsatian	Mr C. Ogley	CC of Lincolnshire	Mr D. Needham
PD	Abbotsway Ringa	B	Boxer	Mrs A. M. West	Mrs A. M. West	Mr T. Yeouart

Stake	*Dog*	*Sex*	*Breed*	*Handler*	*Owner*	*Judge*
TD	Pressburg Zorro	D	Alsatian	PC J. Duff	CC of Surrey	Lady Simpson
TD	Zenda of Stroan	B	Alsatian	Mr J. Etheridge	CC of Lincolnshire	Mrs G. M. Barrington
TD	Hankley Andromeda	B	Alsatian	Mrs D. Foreman	Mrs D. Foreman	Mr W. Chadwick
PD	Pressburg Zorro	D	Alsatian	PC J. Duff	CC of Surrey	Mr R. J. Ling and Mr E. A. Rossiter
	1964					
TD	Zenda of Stroan	B	Alsatian	Mr J. Etheridge	CC of Lincolnshire	Mr R. Matchell
TD	Karadoc Zanella	B	Labrador	Mrs J. S. Mason	Mr and Mrs J. S. Mason	Mrs A. M. West
PD	Pressburgh Zorro	D	Alsatian	PC J. Duff	CC of Surrey	Mr T. Shelton
TD	Karadoc Zanella	B	Labrador	Mrs J. S. Mason	Mr and Mrs J. S. Mason	Mr R. Plumridge
PD	Dagenite Rebel	D	Alsatian	Mr A. Robinson	CC of Lincolnshire	Mr K. Cheetham
TD	Halan Jill	B	Alsatian	Mr H. Allan	Mr H. Allan	Mrs D. Foreman
PD	Vikkas Saracen	D	Alsatian	Mr C. Ogley	CC of Lincolnshire	Capt. P. L. C. Gurney
TD	Harold of Dunmonaidh	D	Alastian	Mr C. Philips	CC of Dundee	Mr T. Sessford
PD	Vikkas Niall	D	Alsatian	Mr W. Darley	CC of Lincolnshire	Mr R. Matchell
TD	Lancon Lucky	D	Alsatian	Mr R. Radford	CC of Lincolnshire	Mr W. Hare

TD	Cassiopeia of Caterdon	B	Alsatian	Mrs L. Davies	Mrs L. Davies	Miss U. Ogle
PD	Arrogant Shane	D	Alsatian	Mr S. Carter	CC of Birmingham	Mr W. Chadwick and Mr R. M. Montgomery
PD	Shane	D	Collie	Miss V. Slatcher	Miss V. Slatcher	Mrs D. Foreman
	1965					
TD	Ballerina of Hankley	B	Alsatian	Mrs D. Foreman	Mrs D. Foreman	Mrs J. Faulks
TD	Petricas Laddie	D	Cross	Mr P. R. Meanwell	Mr and Mrs P. R. Meanwell	Mrs M. Porterfiel
TD	Farnrae Rusty	D	Alsatian	Mr W. Reid	Royal Aircraft Establishment	Mr R. Darbyshire
PD	Shane	D	Collie	Miss V. Slatcher	Miss V. Slatcher	Mr R. Matchell
TD	Orpheus of Hankley	D	Alsatian	Miss U. Ogle	Mrs Foreman and Miss Ogle	Mr T. Shelton
PD	Mountbrowne Wotan	D	Alsatian	PC J. Rebaudi	CC of Nottingham-shire	Mr H. Darbyshire
PD	Vikkas Niall	D	Alsatian	Mr W. Darley	CC of Lincolnshire	Mr T. Yeouart
PD	Petricas Laddie	D	Cross	Mr P. R. Meanwell	Mr and Mrs P. R. Meanwell	Mr D. Needham
PD	Glenroyal of Callender	D	Alsatian	Mr R. Jones	CC of Stoke-on-Trent	Mrs A. M. West
TD	Innsbrook Tatyana	B	Alsatian	PC H. Sibley	CC of Buckinghamshire	Mrs M. Porterfield

Stake	*Dog*	*Sex*	*Breed*	*Handler*	*Owner*	*Judge*
TD	Pibro of Kelso	D	Cross	Mr B. Spooner	Miss J. Allingham	Mrs D. Foreman
PD	Mountbrowne Doron	D	Alsatian	PC S. Wood	CC of Surrey	Mr D. Churchman and Mr. R. Plumridge
TD	Farnrae Rusty	D	Alsatian	Mr W. Reid	Royal Aircraft Establishment	Mr R. Matchell
	1966					
TD	Halan Jill	B	Alsatian	Mr H. Allan	Mr H. Allan	Mr J. Cree
TD	Master of Lawrence	D	Alsatian	Mr J. Newman	Mr J. Newman	Mr W. Redwood
TD	Mountbrowne Wotan	D	Alsatian	PC J. Rebaudi	CC of Nottinghamshire	Mrs J. Faulks
TD	Linnifold Blarney	B	Labrador	Mrs J. S. Mason	Mr and Mrs J. S. Mason	Mr K. Butler
PD	Marcus of Hankley	D	Alsatian	Mr J. Bush	Mrs D. Foreman	Mr R. Plumridge
PD	Jacopo of Aycliffe	D	Alsatian	Mr N. Collyer	CC of the North Riding	Mr G. Wraight
PD	Bowesmoor Bera	D	Alsatian	Mr F. Jordan	CC of the West Midlands	Mr H. Darbyshire
TD	Seal of Polinsa	D	Alsatian	Mr J. Grant	Mr J. Grant	Mr W. E. Reid
PD	Emporor of Catchgate	D	Alsatian	PC J. Clamping	CC of Northampton	Mr K. Cheetham
TD	Hendrawen Olgar	B	Alsatian	Mrs A. M. Dews	Mrs A. M. Dews	Mr T. Yeouart

TD	Hawk of Trevellos	D	Alsatian	Mr H. E. Appleby	Mr H. E. Appleby	Mr T. Shelton
PD	Mountbrowne Ajax	D	Alsatian	PC J. Holloway	CC of Southampton	Mrs D. Foreman and Mr J. Bush
TD	Ob. Ch. Bright Future	D	Alsatian	Mr W. Highcock	Mr and Mrs W. Highcock	Mr J. Bostock
	1967					
TD	Mountbrowne Ajax	D	Alsatian	PC J. Holloway	CC of Southampton	Mr J. Cree
TD	Pride of Alken	B	Alsatian	Mr K. Foster	Mr K. Foster	Mr H. E. Appleby
TD	Farnrae Rusty	D	Alsatian	Mr W. E. Reid	Mr. W. E. Reid	Mr M. B. Davies
TD	Silver of the Drift	B	Alsatian	Mr T. Moore	Mr T. Moore	Mr T. Kane
TD	Lenlee Gladiator	D	R'weiler	Mrs S. M. Osborne	Mrs S. M. Osborne	Mr Rossiter
TD	Mountbrowne Doron	D	Alsatian	PS S. Wood	CC of Surrey	Mr J. Bostock
PD	Jacopo of Aycliffe	D	Alsatian	Mr N. Collyer	CC of North Riding	Mr R. Darbyshire
PD	Prince of Verulam	D	Alsatian	Mr J. Patrick	CC of Sussex	Mr W. Hare
PD	Dirk of Caddam	D	Alsatian	Mr A. Scrimgeour	CC of City of Glasgow	Mr K. Cheetham
PD	Hero of Hasterhill	D	Alsatian	Mr P. M. Ostick	Mr P. M. Ostick	Mr R. Plumridge
TD	Mountbrowne Huntz	D	Alsatian	PC B. Benstead	CC of Surrey	Mr W. Reid
TD	Linnifold Loughderg Churchman	D	Labrador	Mrs J. S. Mason	Mr and Mrs J. S. Mason	Mr P. Thrasher

Stake	*Dog*	*Sex*	*Breed*	*Handler*	*Owner*	*Judge*
TD	Prince of Bournepol	D	Alsatian	PC P. Thrasher	CC of Bournemouth	Mr T. Shelton
PD	Lenlee Gladiator	D	R'weiler	Mrs S. M. Osborne	Mrs S. M. Osborne	Maj. R. J. Clifford and Mr T. Shelton
	1968					
TD	Bowesmoor Jago	D	Alsatian	Mr T. Yeouart	CC of Surrey	Mrs A M. West
TD	Hero of Hastehill	D	Alsatian	Mr P. M. Ostick	Mr P. M. Ostick	Mr D. Needham
PD	Mountbrowne Huntz	D	Alsatian	PC B. Benstead	CC of Surrey	Mr R. J. Ling
TD	Atstan Outlaw	D	Alsatian	Mr B. Hall	Mr and Mrs B. Hall	Mr H. Appleby
TD	Pibro of Kelso	D	Cross	Mr B. Spooner	Miss J. Allingham	Mr J. Bostock
PD	Allessandro of Jugoland	D	Alsatian	Mr K. Christer	CC of Lincolnshire	Mr T. Kane
PD	Seal of Polinsa	D	Alsatian	Mr J. H. Grant	Mr J. H. Grant	Mr W. E. Reid
TD	Victor of Aycliffe	D	Alsatian	Mr J. Dykes	CC of Dundee	Sgt J. Todd
PD	Glenroyal of Callander	D	Alsatian	Mr R. Jones	CC of Stoke-on-Trent	Mr W. E. Reid
TD	Linnifold Blarney	B	Labrador	Mrs J. S. Mason	Mr and Mrs J. S. Mason	Mr R. Plumridge
PD	Prince of Hogganfield	D	Alsatian	Mr A. Moyies	CC of City of Glasgow	Mr K. Cheetham
TD	Laddie of Clan Dhai	D	Alsatian	PC Murphy	CC of the British Transport Police	Mr F. K. Butler

PD	Hero of Hastehill	D	Alsatian	Mr P. M. Ostick	Mr P. M. Ostick	Mr R. Matchell and Sgt Wood
	1969					
TD	Hero of Hastehill	D	Alsatian	Mr P. M. Ostick	Mr P. M. Ostick	Mr H. Appleby
TD	Linnifold Blarney	B	Labrador	Mrs J. S. Mason	Mr and Mrs J. S. Mason	Mr W. Hare
TD	Shane of Invajendra	D	Alsatian	Mr J. Allen	Mr and Mrs J. Allen	Mr B. Ling
TD	Innsbrook Tatyana	B	Alsatian	Mr H. Sibley	CC of Thames Valley	Mr W. Reid
TD	Ob. Ch. Micklyn Shandy	D	Cross	Mrs J. M. McMillan	Mrs J. M. McMillan	Mr R. Plumridge
PD	Hero of Hastehill	D	Alsatian	Mr P. Ostick	Mr P. Ostick	Mr W. Reid
TD	Ob. Ch. Micklyn Whisky	D	Collie	Mrs J. M. McMillan	Mrs J. M. McMillan	Mr P. C. Thrasher
PD	Victor of Aycliffe	D	Alsatian	Mr J. Dykes	CC of City of Dundee	Sgt C. Ogley
PD	Petricas Laddie	D	Cross	Mr P. R. Meanwell	Mr and Mrs P. R. Meanwell	Mr A. Howard
PD	Victor of Aycliffe	D	Alsatian	Mr J. Dykes	CC of Dundee	Mr D. Hare
PD	Dewley of Northumbria	D	Alsatian	Mr J. Boyd	CC of West Yorkshire	Mrs A. M. West
TD	Linnifold Blarney	B	Labrador	Mrs J. S. Mason	Mr and Mrs J. S. Mason	Mr C. Brockett
PD	Barimilne The Warlord	D	Alsatian	Mr F. Jolley	Commissioner of City of London Police	Mr R. Plumridge and Mr Rossiter
TD	Petricas Laddie	D	Cross	Mr P. R. Meanwell	Mr and Mrs P. R. Meanwell	Mr W. Reid

Stake	*Dog*	*Sex*	*Breed*	*Handler*	*Owner*	*Judge*
	1970					
TD	Manymills Tanne	B	Labrador	Mrs S. Pickup	Mrs S. Pickup	Mr B. M. Davies
TD	Beedawn Liza	B	Alsatian	Mr A. E. Hutchinson	Mr A. E. Hutchinson	Sgt G. Grayson
TD	Kingsmens Cobbler	D	Alsatian	Mr F. McCarthy	Mr F. McCarthy	Mr P. R. Meanwell
PD	Hero of Hastehill	D	Alsatian	Mr P. M. Ostick	Mr P. M. Ostick	Mr R. Matchell
TD	Atstan Outlaw	D	Alsatian	Mr B. Hall	Mr B. Hall	Mr B. M. Davies
TD	Arkwood of Amberwell	D	Alsatian	Mrs M. Y. Fisk	Mrs M. Y. Fisk	Mr H. Darbyshire
TD	Linnifold Blarney	B	Labrador	Mrs J. S. Mason	Mrs J. S. Mason	Mr B. Spooner
PD	Highlight of Croftwood	D	Alsatian	Mr D. Knowling	Mr D. Knowling	Mr D. Needham
PD	Hero of Hastehill	D	Alsatian	Mr P. M. Ostick	Mr P. M. Ostick	Mr G. Wraight
TD	Uberalles Klein	D	Alsatian	Mr W. Hunter	CC of Dundee	Mr C. Ogley
TD	Shane of Invajendra	D	Alsatian	Mr J. Allen	Mr and Mrs J. Allen	PC P. Thrasher and Sgt S. Wood
PD	Invader of Hankley	D	Alsatian	Mr F. C. Bell	Mr F. C. Bell	Mr K. Cheetham
TD	Kingsmens Cobbler	D	Alsatian	Mr F. McCarthy	Mr F. McCarthy	Mrs A. M. West
TD	Arkwood of Amberwell	D	Alsatian	Mrs Y. Fisk	Mrs Y. Fisk	Mr H. Appleby
PD	Nikki of Hankley	D	Alsatian	Mr F. C. Bell	Mr F. C. Bell	Mrs D. Foreman and Mr W. Chadwick

TD	Kingsmens Cobbler	D	Alsatian	Mr F. McCarthy	Mr F. McCarthy	Mr G. Dunsdon
	1971					
TD	Leo of Perrycourt	D	Alsatian	Mr J. Hudson	Mr J. Hudson	Mr R. Ling
TD	Hill Billy Boy	D	Labrador	Mr P. D. W. Lewis	Mr P. D. W. Lewis	Mr R. Spooner
TD	Ardfern Bruar	B	Alsatian	Mr D. M. Clark	Mr D. M. Clark	Mrs J. Faulks
TD	Mannymills Tanne	B	Labrador	Mrs S. G. Pickup	Mrs S. G. Pickup	Mr P. R. Meanwell
TD	Invader of Hankley	D	Alsatian	Mr F. C. Bell	Mr F. C. Bell	Mr W. Hare
TD	Linnifold Blarney	D	Labrador	Mrs J. S. Mason	Mr and Mrs J. S. Mason	Sgt S. Wood
PD	Wesmid Bowesmoor Gerald	D	Alsatian	Mr G. Garbutt	CC of the West Midlands	Mr P. Thrasher
PD	Petricas Laddie	D	Cross	Mr P. R. Meanwell	Mr and Mrs P. R. Meanwell	Mr C. Ogley
PD	Petricas Laddie	D	Cross	Mr P. R. Meanwell	Mr and Mrs P. R. Meanwell	Sgt G. Grayson
PD	Petricas Laddie	D	Cross	Mr P. R. Meanwell	Mrr and Mrs P. R. Meanwell	Mrs A. M. West
TD	Farmers Rob	D	Sheepdog	Mr E. R. Skeates	Mr E. R. Skeates	Mr D. Churchman and Mr C. Brockett
PD	Wesmid Bowesmoor Gerald	D	Alsatian	PC G. Garbutt	CC of the West Midlands	Mr R. Ling
TD	Barrimilne Saba	D	Alsatian	Mr G. Wraight	CC of the Thames Police	Mr R. Darbyshire

Stake	*Dog*	*Sex*	*Breed*	*Handler*	*Owner*	*Judge*
TD	Invader of Hankley	D	Alsatian	Mr F. C. Bell	Mr F. C. Bell	Mr B. M. Davies
PD	Perticas Laddie	D	Cross	Mr P. R. Meanwell	Mr and Mrs P. R. Meanwell	Sgt J. Bostock
TD	Linnifold Blarney	D	Labrador	Mrs J. S. Mason	Mr and Mrs J. S. Mason	Sgt G. Dunsdon and Mr A. Wheatley
	1972					
TD	Knocknaman Paddy	D	Cross	Mrs R. Parker	Mrs R. Parker	Mr D. Scott
TD	Linnifold Witchcraft	B	Labrador	Mrs A. C. Mason	Mrs A. C. Mason	Mr H. Appleby
TD	Skipper Crusader	D	Alsatian	Mr B. Plant	CC of the Thames Valley	Mr W. Champion
TD	Barrimilne Saba	D	Alsatian	Mr G. Wraight	CC of the Thames Valley	Mr W. Ramsey
TD	Scott of Pravey	D	Cross	Mr M. Davey	Mr M. Davey	Mr P. B. Joyce
PD	Moorland Mystic	D	Sheepdog	Mr D. Storey	Mr D. Storey	Mr G. Grayson
TD	Beedawn Liza	D	Alsatian	Mr A. Hutchinson	Mr A. Hutchinson	Mr S. A. Emmerson
TD	Greyvalley Grock	D	Alsatian	Mr M. J. Jones	Mr M. J. Jones	Mr P. D. W. Lewis
PD	Dunelm Rebel	D	Alsatian	Mr F. Collins	CC of Lincolnshire	Insp J. Hyslop
TD	Petricas Laddie	D	Cross	Mr P. R. Meanwell	Mr and Mrs P. R. Meanwell	Mr A. Scrimgeour
TD	Farmers Rob	D	Sheepdog	Mr E. R. Skeates	Mr E. R. Skeates	Sgt C. Ogley and PC P. Thrasher

TD	Nikki of Hankley	D	Alsatian	Mr F. C. Bell	Mr F. C. Bell	Mr R. Wood
PD	Wydawake Leo	D	Alsatian	Mr L. Oldfield	Mr L. Oldfield	Mr P. R. Meanwell
PD	Wesmid Bowesmoor Gerald	D	Alsatian	Mr G. Garbutt	CC of West Midlands	Mr B. M. Davies
TD	Beedawn Liza	B	Alsatian	Mr A. E. Hutchinson	Mr A. E. Hutchinson	Mr J. Bostock
PD	Invader of Hankley	D	Alsatian	Mr F. C. Bell	Mr F. C. Bell	Mr D. Churchman
TD	Invader of Hankley	D	Alsatian	Mr F. C. Bell	Mr F. C. Bell	Sgt R. Plumridge and Sgt G. Cordrey
	1973					
TD	Scott of Pravey	D	Cross	Mr M. Davey	Mr M. Davey	Mr P. D. W. Lewis
TD	Bowesmoor Falk	D	Alsatian	Mr E. T. Hadley	Mr E. T. Hadley	Mr C. Brockett
TD	Moorland Mystic	D	Sheepdog	Mr D. Storey	Mr D. Storey	Sgt S. Carter
TD	Scott of Pravey	D	Cross	Mr M. Davey	Mr M. Davey	Mr R. Darbyshire
TD	Tanfield Wystan	D	Alsatian	PC E. T. Buckle	CC City of London	Mr J. Bostock
TD	Nyewoods Charlie Boy	D	Sheepdog	Mr D. Rutter	Mr D. Rutter	Mr R. Plumridge
PD	Nikki of Hankley	D	Alsatian	Mr F. C. Bell	Mr F. C. Bell	Mr S. C. Wood
PD	Amber of Brayfield	B	Alsatian	Mr P. R. Meanwell	Mr and Mrs P. R. Meanwell	Mr P. Thrasher
PD	Nikki of Hankley	D	Alsatian	Mr F. C. Bell	Mr F. C. Bell	Mr W. Redwood
PD	Farmers Rob	D	Sheepdog	Mr E. R. Skeates	Mr E. R. Skeates	Mr J. Todd

Stake	*Dog*	*Sex*	*Breed*	*Handlers*	*Owner*	*Judge*
TD	Tanfield Millflash Parro	D	Alsatian	Mr B. Hall	Mr B. Hall	Mr J. Comber and Mr R. Spooner
TD	Greyvalley Grock	D	Alsatian	Mr M. J. Jones	Mr M. J. Jones	P Ins G. Grayson
PD	Moorland Mystic	D	Sheepdog	Mr D. Storey	Mr D. Storey	Mr H. E. Appleby
TD	Moolen Unus	B	Alsatian	Mr E. T. Senior	Mr E. T. Senior	Mr R. Spooner
TD	Linnifold Witchcraft	B	Labrador	Mrs A. C. Mason	Mrs A. C. Mason	Mr P. R. Meanwell
TD	Moorland Mystic	D	Sheepdog	Mr D. Storey	Mr D. Storey	Mr D. Churchman and Mr N. Haydock
PD	Nikki of Hankley	D	Alsatian	Mr F. C. Bell	Mr F. C. Bell	Mr P. R. Meanwell
TD	Ashwood Ben	D	Collie	Mr T. Jones	Mr T. Jones	Mr H. Darbyshire
	1974					
TD	Bowesmoor Falk	D	Alsatian	Mr E. T. Hadley	Mr E. T. Hadley	Mr H. Appleby
TD	Greyvalley Grock	D	Alsatian	Mr M. Jones	Mr M. Jones	Mr R. Ling
PD	Caruso of Mountholm	D	Alsatian	Mr C. Young	Mr C. Young	Mr R. Darbyshire
TD	Bois of Limbrook	D	Alsatian	PC K. Lake	Commissioner of the Metropolitan Police	Mr R. Plumridge
TD	Tessa of Thornymoor	B	Collie	Mrs D. Cowley	Mrs D. Cowley	Mr R. Spooner
TD	Night Raider of Invajendra	D	Alsatian	Mrs J. Allen	Mrs J. Allen	Mr B. Hall

PD	Tanfield Wystan	D	Alsatian	PC E. T. Buckle	Commissioner of the City of London Police	Mr A. Scrimgeour
PD	Tanfield Wystan	D	Alsatian	PC E. T. Buckle	Commissioner of the City of London Police	Mr D. Churchman
TD	Ashwood Ben	D	Collie	Mr T. Jones	Mr T. Jones	Mr G. Wraight
PD	Bois of Limbrook	D	Alsatian	PC K. Lake	Commissioner of the Metropolitan Police	Mrs A. M. West
TD	Glaspol Wallsdale Zodiac	D	Alsatian	Mr J. Bennett	CC Glasgow	Mr J. Cree
PD	Jerisquad Axel	D	Alsatian	PC E. Simpson	CC of Durham	Mr B. M. Davies
PD	Moorland Mystic	D	Sheepdog	Mr D. Storey	Mr D. Storey	Mr P. R. Meanwell
TD	Tanfield Wystan	D	Alsatian	PC E. T. Buckle	Commissioner of the City of London Police	Mr W. Reid
TD	Moorland Mystic	D	Sheepdog	Mr D. Storey	Mr D. Storey	Mr G. Cordrey
PD	Tanfield Wystan	D	Alsatian	PC E. T. Buckle	Commissioner of the City of London Police	Mr J. Bostock
TD	Greyvalley Grock	D	Alsatian	Mr M. Jones	Mr M. Jones	Mr H. Appleby
TD	Bois of Limbrook	D	Alsatian	PC K. Lake	Commissioner of the Metropolitan Police	Mr W. McGorrigan

Stake	Dog	Sex	Breed	Handler	Owner	Judge
	1975					
TD	Tanfield Millflash Parro	D	Alsatian	Mr B. Hall	Mr B. Hall	Mr P. Meanwell
PD	Tanfield Wystan	D	Alsatian	Mr E. T. Buckle	Mr E. T. Buckle	Mr W. Champion
TD	Ashwood Ben	D	Collie	Mr T. Jones	Mr T. Jones	Mr J. Cree
TD	Tanfield Wystan	D	Alsatian	Mr E. T. Buckle	Mr E. T. Buckle	Mr W. Ramsey
TD	Tessa of Thornymoor	B	Collie	Mrs D. Cowley	Mrs D. Cowley	Mr B. M. Davies
TD	Night Raider of Invajendra	D	Alsatian	Mr J. Allen	Mr J. Allen	Mr S. C. Wood
TD	Linnifold Black Magic	B	Labrador	Mrs S. Hodson	Mrs S. Hodson	Mr C. Ogley
TD	Tap	D	Collie	Mr P. D. W. Lewis	Mr P. D. W. Lewis	Mr R. Spooner
PD	Tanfield Wystan	D	Alsatian	Mr E. T. Buckle	Mr E. T. Buckle	Mr R. Plumridge
PD	Bowesmoor Falk	D	Alsatian	Mr T. Hadley	Mr T. Hadley	Mr P. Ostick
PD	Moorland Mystic	D	Collie	Mr D. Storey	Mr D. Storey	Mr F. Jolley
PD	Jamie of Petricas	D	Sheepdog	Mr P. Meanwell	Mr P. Meanwell	Mr R. Wood
TD	Metpol Fang	D	Alsatian	PC G. Luck-Baker	Commissioner of the Metropolitan Police	Mr T. Shelton
TD	Taypol Amalga	D	Alsatian	PS J. Dykes	CC Tayside	Mr J. Hislop
TD	Tessa of Thornymoor	B	Collie	Mrs D. Cowley	Mrs D. Cowley	Mrs S. M. Buckle

PD	Bois of Limbrook	D	Alsatian	PC K. Lake	Commissioner of the Metropolitan Police	Mr R. Ling
PD	Bois of Limbrook	D	Alsatian	PC K. Lake	Commissioner of the Metropolitan Police	Mr W. Redwood
TD	Linnifold Black Magic	B	Labrador	Mrs S. Hodson	Mrs S. Hodson	Mr J. Cree
PD	Bois of Limbrook	D	Alsatian	PC K. Lake	Commissioner of the Metropolitan Police	Mr J. Dykes
TD	Linnifold Black Magic	B	Labrador	Mrs S. Hodson	Mrs S. Hodson	Mr C. Brockett
	1976					
TD	Devcornpol Czar	D	Alsatian	PS P. Broad	CC Devon & Cornwall	Mr B. Hall
PD	Holtbeck Max	D	Sheepdog	Mr G. Halford	Mr G. Halford	Mr C. Ogley
TD	Wandering Star of Kenstaff	D	Alsatian	PC A. Moss	CC Hertfordshire	Mrs A. West
TD	Burnaway Freia	B	Alsatian	Mrs S. Hardaway	Mrs S. Hardaway	Mrs J. Faulks
TD	Lance of Amberwell	D	Alsatian	Mr M. J. Jones	Mr M. J. Jones	Mr R. Spooner
TD	Tap	D	Collie	Mr P. D. W. Lewis	Mr P. D. W. Lewis	Mr W. Ramsey
TD	Lance of Amberwell	D	Alsatian	Mr M. J. Jones	Mr M. J. Jones	Mr T. Shelton
PD	Bois of Limbrook	D	Alsatian	PC K. Lake	Commissioner of the Metropolitan Police	Mr P. Meanwell
TD	Bowesmoor Hugo	D	Alsatian	Mr D. Barwick	Mr D. Barwick	Mr M. Jones
PD	Tanfield Wystan	D	Alsatian	Mr E. T. Buckle	Mr E. T. Buckle	Mr J. Bostock

Stake	*Dog*	*Sex*	*Breed*	*Handler*	*Owner*	*Judge*
TD	Glaspol Shane	D	Alsatian	Mr M. Ford	CC of Strathclyde	Mr R. Darbyshire
PD	Tanfield Wystan	D	Alsatian	Mr E. T. Buckle	Mr E. T. Buckle	Sgt D. Davies
PD	Dalynmar Admiral	D	Alsatian	Mr L. J. Tucker	Mr L. J. Tucker	Mr G. Grayson
TD	Marhaba of Berryfield	B	I. W'hound	Miss J. Milnes	Miss J. Milnes	Mr J. Cree
TD	Millfoyle Milford	D	Alsatian	PC G. Dunsdon	CC of Dorset	Mr D. Churchman and Mr J. Allen
PD	Taypol Amalga	D	Alsatian	PS J. Dyke	CC Tayside	Mr G. Wraight
PD	Bowesmoor Hugo	D	Alsatian	Mr D. Barwick	Mr D. Barwick	Mr J. Thomson
TD	Bowesmoor Hugo	D	Alsatian	Mr D. Barwick	Mr D. Barwick	Mr H. Radford
TD	Burnaway Freia	B	Alsatian	Mrs S. Hardaway	Mrs S. Hardaway	Mr W. Champion and Mr A. Wheatley
TD	Neypol Djai	D	Alsatian	PC J. Birks	CC North Yorkshire	Mr C. Ogley
PD	Dalynmar Admiral	D	Alsatian	Mr L. Tucker	Mr L. Tucker	Mr R. Wood
TD	Linnifold Black Magic	B	Labrador	Mrs S. Hodson	Mrs S. Hodson	Mr R. Plumridge
PD	Jamie of Petricas	D	Collie	Mr P. Meanwell	Mr P. Meanwell	Mr S. C. Wood
PD	Dalynmar Admiral	D	Alsatian	Mr L. Tucker	Mr L. Tucker	Mr F. Jolley

Index